T0325081

The Zero Trust Framework

The Cybersecurity landscape is a daunting one today. It is nothing like it was 10 years ago. Now, it has become very complex, covert, dynamic, and stealthy. It has literally become a cat and mouse game, in which the Cyberattacker is still one step ahead. This is despite all of the technology that is available to us as a society, which includes Artificial Intelligence (AI) and Machine Learning.

Part of the other problem is that human beings are resistant to change. For example, the password is still the favored way of authenticating and authorizing an individual, but it too has shown its grave limitations. Despite the use of Password Managers, which can create long and complex passwords, people still resort to their old fashioned ways of doing things.

So, what is needed now is an extreme change, in which, unfortunately, people have no choice in whether or not they will participate. It is called the Zero Trust Framework, and in this methodology, absolutely nobody can be trusted in either the internal or the external environments. The mantra here is to keep verifying everybody, all the time.

The Zero Trust Framework also involves the concept of segmentation, in which the IT and Network Infrastructure of a business is broken down into smaller components, much like a Subnet. Each component will have its own layer of security, and every individual must be authenticated via the use of Multifactor Authentication (MFA).

In this book, we review both the concepts and mechanics behind the Zero Trust Framework. We also introduce advanced technologies into it, including the use of Biometrics, the Public Key Infrastructure, and Quantum Mechanics/Quantum Cryptography.

Ravindra Das is a Cybersecurity Consultant with his own practice, RaviDas. Tech, Inc. (ravidas.consulting). He is Certified in Cybersecurity by the ISC(2), has written and published 9 books with CRC Press, and self-published 24 eBooks on Amazon. His portfolio can be seen at: cybersecuritycontent.news

The Zero Trust Framework
Threat Hunting & Quantum Mechanics

Ravindra Das

CRC Press
Taylor & Francis Group
Boca Raton   London   New York

CRC Press is an imprint of the
Taylor & Francis Group, an **informa** business

First edition published 2024
by CRC Press
6000 Broken Sound Parkway NW, Suite 300, Boca Raton, FL 33487-2742

and by CRC Press
4 Park Square, Milton Park, Abingdon, Oxon, OX14 4RN

© 2024 Ravindra Das

CRC Press is an imprint of Taylor & Francis Group, LLC

Library of Congress Cataloging-in-Publication Data
Names: Das, Ravindra, author.
Title: The zero trust framework : threat hunting & quantum mechanics /
Ravindra Das.
Description: First edition. | Boca Raton : CRC Press, [2024] | Includes
bibliographical references and index.
Identifiers: LCCN 2023006003 (print) | LCCN 2023006004 (ebook) | ISBN
9781032492780 (hardback) | ISBN 9781032492810 (paperback) | ISBN
9781003392965 (ebook)
Subjects: LCSH: Computer networks--Security measures. | Computer security.
| Trust. | Internet users--Identification.
Classification: LCC TK5105.59 .D3738 2024 (print) | LCC TK5105.59 (ebook)
| DDC 005.8--dc23/eng/20230228
LC record available at https://lccn.loc.gov/2023006003
LC ebook record available at https://lccn.loc.gov/2023006004

ISBN: 978-1-032-49278-0 (hbk)
ISBN: 978-1-032-49281-0 (pbk)
ISBN: 978-1-003-39296-5 (ebk)

DOI: 10.1201/9781003392965

Typeset in Times
by SPi Technologies India Pvt Ltd (Straive)

This book is dedicated to my Lord and Savior, Jesus Christ, the Grand Designer of the Universe, and to my parents, Dr. Gopal Das and Mrs. Kunda Das.

This book is also dedicated to:
Richard and Gwenda Bowman
Anita Bhalla Das and Mary Hanlon Bhalla
Tim Auckley and his family
My loving cats, Fifi and Bubu

Contents

Acknowledgments

I would like to thank Ms. Gabriella Williams, my editor, who made this book into a reality.

Introduction

1

The world of Cybersecurity is now a complex one. Gone are the days when it was all just about Phishing attacks like in the late 90s. Now it is a myriad of threat vectors, psychological tactics, and essentially digital warfare among nations and its peoples. Unfortunately, as time goes on, this is only going to get worse. This is best exemplified by the conflict between Russia and the Ukraine. This war has been going on for almost a year now, with no end in sight.

True, there are the military machines of war present. But now, there is a twist – Cyberattacks being launched against the Ukrainians by the Russians. Never has this happened before in the history of warfare. In fact, it is expected that even future wars will be fought mostly on the digital front, as there will be no further need for the physical armor to be present.

Even future terrorist attacks will not involve airplanes crashing into buildings like we saw during 9/11. Now, it will be a series of large-scale Cyberattacks aimed at the Critical Infrastructures of any one country. These will be simultaneous attacks aimed towards the oil and gas pipelines, water supplies, the food distribution system, the national power grid, and even the nuclear facilities of a country, literally bringing it down to its knees.

Even though the threat variants have become much more dangerous and covert and even stealthier, so has the advancements been made in the various security technologies and tools that are designed to protect not only businesses but also individuals. For example, the tools of Artificial Intelligence and Machine Learning are now being used to speed and automate processes that would take days to achieve. Now, these tools are used to comb through large amounts of data in order to unearth any hidden trends that could prove to be useful for any IT Security team.

To some degree, they are also being used to predict what the future Cyber Threat Landscape could potentially look like, as well as what the threat variants could be. But, it should be noted that these tools are only as good as the data that is being fed into them. In other words, garbage in and garbage out. Intelligence sharing has also greatly increased, between both the private and government sectors. This has proven to be of great benefit, as the FBI has been

DOI: 10.1201/9781003392965-1

able to take some of the most notorious Ransomware groups, and even retrieve the money that was paid as ransom to the hackers.

But even despite all of this, it still seems like that it is not enough. The crux of the problem here is that businesses in Corporate America are simply way too reactive. The attitude seems to be of this: "If it has not hit me yet, the chances are that it will never happen". This is the main reason why people are so ignorant about security issues. The other piece of the puzzle that is often left to blame here in this regard is the cost of implementing security controls.

True, it can be a very exhaustive and time-constraining activity to conduct a Risk Assessment, but the truth of the matter is that security controls are now very affordable today, especially to the small- and medium-sized business (SMBs). Another problem here is that the primary tool that is used for authentication as well as authorization has been and continues to be the traditional password.

There have been many advances made in password security, especially that of the Password Manager. For example, it can create very long and complex passwords that are almost very difficult to break. It can even remind employees of when they need to reset their passwords, or it can even do it automatically for them. It can also alert the employee if their password has been compromised in any way. Even despite all of this, people are still afraid to use, just because this will mean a change in the routines in which things are done. By nature, humans are very resistant to change, and this is a part of the reason of why the Cyberattacker can still carry the way they do. This is an issue that will be further addressed in Chapter 6.

Thus, the only way to guarantee that a business or an individual can be mitigated as much as possible from a security breach is to take extreme measures of all kinds. One such example of this is known as the "Zero Trust Framework". In this methodology, absolutely nobody or anything is to be trusted in both the external and the internal environments. People simply cannot use their passwords anymore in order to gain access to the resources that they need to conduct in their everyday job functions.

Instead, employees must be constantly verified all of the time, going through at least three or more layers of proving and confirming their identities. Also, the IT and Network Infrastructure of an organization is broken down into different layers or segments, in order to make sure that the Cyberattacker cannot break through any further. The thinking here is that if the Cyberattacker can break through the first lines of defenses, the chances that they can break through the other, subsequent ones become almost nil.

This is a far cry from the traditional approaches, which were called the Perimeter Defense Model. With this kind of methodology, a business was surrounded by just one layer of defense, in a circle. Although this would have been heavily fortified, but if the Cyberattacker were to break through, they would then literally have free reigns over all of the digital assets of the company.

In this regard, the Zero Trust Framework can totally super cede the Perimeter Defense Model, with all of the internal layers of security that it consists of. Although the Zero Trust Framework is once again viewed as an extreme, this is what is needed today to thwart off the Cyberattackers to the greatest degrees possible.

Although this methodology has been around for quite some time (around 10 years or so), it is not until now that it has been formally adopted to varying degrees. But for the most part, there has been success rate with it, as it has been more difficult for the Cyberattacker to penetrate into.

Thus, the primary goal of this book is to review the Zero Trust Framework, and how it can be possibly deployed even at your organization. But in this regard, we break away from the traditional Zero Trust Framework Model, and incorporate three new facets into it:

- The use of Biometric Technology;
- The Use of Quantum Mechanics;
- The Use of Asymmetric Key Cryptography, also known as the Public Key Infrastructure, or the PKI.

The Fundamental Components of the Zero Trust Framework

2

In the world of security, not just Cybersecurity, the identification of an individual is not just a requirement these days, but it is an absolute must. But the ways about going to conduct this identification process vary from company to company; some require multiple layers of it, and some just require one mechanism in order to fully confirm the identity of the person in question (this will be discussed in detail later on in this chapter). Probably, the most traditional way of confirming somebody has been the password.

THE PASSWORD

In fact, the password is the dinosaur of identification, having gone back decades. It certainly has proved its identity over time, but now, given the sophistication of the Cyberattacker, it has literally outlived its usefulness. A primary reason for this is that this is a much sought after prize for the hacker, because after all, once they have a password, all they need to do is somehow guess the username (unless they already have from a previous security breach).

Once this has been accomplished, then their reign of terror can begin. For example, they can drain your bank accounts, and even launch credit card fraud attacks (the author of this chapter has actually been a victim of this). Or, this can be sold on the Dark Web for a rather nice profit, along with the other username/password combinations that have been heisted.

DOI: 10.1201/9781003392965-2

Or in a new trend that is happening these days is that the Cyberattacker can actually hire out another firm on the Dark Web and have them launch on attack using the stolen credentials. This has become known as a "Ransomware as a Service" attack. But even though the password has been such a huge target, many people still choose to keep on doing things associated with it as they normally have.

Instead of heeding the warnings of their employers, many people do the following with their passwords:

1) They reuse the same password across multiple platforms;
2) When it is time to reset the password, rather than coming up with something different, they use just slightly different alteration of the original password;
3) They will use a very easy-to-remember password; some of the following are typical examples that have been used and continue to do so:
   - Password
   - 123456
   - 123456789
   - 12345678
   - 1234567
   - Password1
   - 12345
   - 1234567890
   - 1234
   - Qwerty123
4) They will use other forms to create an easy-to-remember password, such as a birthdate, name of a relative, or even the name of a previous employer. Now, these are obviously a little bit more secure to use that the passwords listed in #3, but they are still very easy to guess, given the use of OSINT (also known as Open Source Intelligence), and the availability of Social Media profiles.

Because of this, almost 99% of all business in Corporate America have now mandated that their employees come up with a much stronger password, one that is much harder to crack and break into. Some of the guidelines for creating these kinds of passwords include the following:

1) Keep the password long. Many Cyber vendors recommend creating a password at least 15 to 16 characters long, and this should be interspersed with punctuation, numerical values, and upper and lower case letters.
2) Avoid substitutions from previous passwords. The reason for this is because there is a very strong possibility that the older one could

have been hijacked in a previous security breach, and if it is altered in just a slight way, it could still very well be detected in a later, brute force attack. An example of substitutions include the following:

DOORBELL becoming D00R8377

3) Be careful of using keyboard shortcuts. If you have any key logger spyware maliciously deployed on your wireless device, it can track these movements very easily and send them back to the Cyberattacker in a Remote Code Execution (RCE) attack.
4) If you have an existing passphrase created elsewhere, it is recommended that you create a different version of that, using a combination of meaningless words in the process.
5) Another, more superior version of the passphrase is to create a sentence (not too long) as your password. Here is an example:

The Old Duke is my favorite pub in South London
Now becomes
ThOlDuismyfapuinSoLo
(SOURCE: https://blog.avast.com/strong-password-ideas)

Other examples include the following:

2BorNot2B_ThatIsThe? (To be or not to be, that is the question – from Shakespeare)
L8r_L8rNot2day (Later, later, not today – from the kid's rhyme)
4Score&7yrsAgo (Four score and seven years ago – from the Gettysburg Address)
John3:16=4G (Scriptural reference)
14A&A41dumaS (one for all and all for 1 – from The Three Musketeers, by Dumas)
(SOURCE: https://www.webroot.com/us/en/resources/tips-articles/how-do-i-create-a-strong-password)

6) Another recommended way to create a very strong password is to use your favorite websites, or the ones that you visit most commonly. Some typical examples of this include the following:

ABT2_uz_AMZ! (About to use Amazon)
ABT2_uz_BoA! (About to use Bank of America)
Pwrd4Acct-$$ (Password for account at the bank)
Pwrd4Acct-Fb (Password for a Facebook account)
(SOURCE: https://www.webroot.com/us/en/resources/tips-articles/how-do-i-create-a-strong-password)

7) In some places where a complex password is required, you can even create an emoticon. The caveat here is that you can't use the actual image, you can only create one from the symbols that are available on your keyboard. The following matrix displays this:

!
@
#
$
%
^
&
*
(
)
_
+
{
}
|
"
<
>
-
=
[
]
;
\
'
,
.
/

Because these newer versions of passwords are far more complex than the easier ones just listed, people still tend to shy away from using these. The answer is quite simple here, as they are too hard to remember. And that is using the Password Manager.

It can be technically defined as follows:

They store your login information for all the websites you use and help you log into them automatically.

(SOURCE: https://www.howtogeek.com/141500/why-you-should-use-a-password-manager-and-how-to-get-started/)

Essentially, it is a software application package, which comes with the following features:

- It creates long and complex passwords that are hard to crack;
- It stores those passwords;
- It can reset passwords automatically on a preestablished timetable;
- It will keep a track of all the websites that you visit, and store that into its memory;
- It will login into those websites automatically for you;
- It will create passwords for all of the Operating Systems (OS's) that you may be using, including macOS, Windows, Linux, iOS, and Android;
- It will alert you if one your passwords has been hijacked and automatically reset it for you;
- It will even scan the Dark Web for you to make sure that your login credentials do not reside there;
- It can also store your other important documents like your driver's license and insurance card.

To log into a Password Manager, you will need another use another form of authentication, such as a One Type Password (OTP) or something similar to an RSA Token. The former is sent to you as a text on your smartphone. But even despite all of this, unless their job is dependent upon it, employees still even ignore to use this tool. Instead, they would much rather use an easy-to-remember password, or if they have to remember a long and complex password, they will simply write it down next to their monitor, which will be available in plain sight.

So, what can be done to rectify all of this, if the password is still to be used? This is where the role of Two-Factor Authentication, also known as "2FA", comes into play.

THE RISE OF TWO-FACTOR AUTHENTICATION

The last section just reviewed how passwords have been such a crux in our digital society of today. But no matter how much we acknowledge the great, inherent weaknesses that are in them, and even more so, how much we want to get rid of them, the bottom line is that they will still be here for a long time to come. Despite the recommendation to further strengthen them, just about a majority of the population here in the United States still likes to go back to their old patterns of using passwords, not only putting themselves at a greater risk, but the people around them as well.

So, the best that can be done here is to build a better mousetrap for authentication, while still using the password. So how does one go about this? Well it comes down to using another authentication tool along with the password. As mentioned earlier, it can range from using a challenge/answer response question to using a smart card. This has now become known as "Two Factor Authentication", or simply known as "2FA". It can be technically defined as follows:

> Two-factor authentication (2FA) is an identity and access management security method that requires two forms of identification to access resources and data. 2FA gives businesses the ability to monitor and help safeguard their most vulnerable information and networks.
> *(SOURCE: https://www.microsoft.com/en-us/security/business/*
> *security-101/what-is-two-factor-authentication-2fa#:~:text=*
> *Two%2Dfactor%20authentication%20(2FA),most%20vulnerable%20*
> *information%20and%20networks)*

Simply put, along with the password with another form of authentication. An example of this is illustrated below:

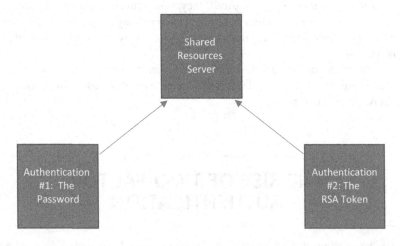

In the above example, the employee is requesting to be authenticated so that he or she can gain access to the server that houses the shared resources that they need to complete a certain project. The first level of authentication is entering a password (no matter how easy or complex it actually is), and the second level of authentication is the RSA Token. Once the employee passes through these two hurdles, they can then be granted access to the server.

The primary aim of using 2FA is obvious: If the Cyber attacker can break through the password, they still have to break through yet another line of defense to get access to the server. And this one will probably prove to be more difficult to crack. There are other types of 2FA tokens, and they include the following:

1) Hardware tokens:
   These are FOBs that produces a brand new, numerical code every few seconds. In fact, the RSA Token works similarly in this manner.
2) Push Notification:
   A One-Time Password (also known as an OTP) is sent as a text message to your smartphone. Most of the time, it is just a five or six number numerical value that you have to enter in the website you are trying to get into. Many financial institutions use this technique as a means of confirming your identity.
3) SMS Verification:
   This is when a legitimate link is sent to your smartphone, and you have to click on it in order to gain access. Amazon makes use of this type of verification before you can gain access to your account.
4) Voice authentication:
   This is a much more advanced technique in that Voice Recognition is being used to confirm your identity. It is also another form of a Biometric-based modality.

Along with the advantages that 2FA brings, it also has a number of key drawbacks as well, which include the following:

1) The user can be locked out:
   Suppose the end user successfully enters in their password, but has difficulty getting passed through the second one. Also assume that this is a legitimate employee as well. This person can be locked after a certain number of unsuccessful attempts (the limit here is usually at three).
2) It can take more time:
   With the technological advancements of today, 2FA should not take more than a few minutes to accomplish. But technology can have certain points of failures, and if the 2FA system is not an optimal working mode, it can take even longer to get access. This only adds more to the frustration level of the end user.

3) It can be complex and expensive:
   For a simple Mom and Pop business, deploying 2FA should be relatively quick and not too expensive. But if you are a Fortune 100 company or so, implementing a 2FA solution can take a much longer time to deploy, and can be much costlier as well, because of the need to hire an outside vendor to the actual deployment.

4) A psychological issue:
   The bottom line is that human beings are creature of habit. Most of the time, we like to do things that we are accustomed to doing it, and don't want any change with it. The same is true of 2FA. It can take a long time for employees to get adjusted to this process, and just one bad experience can negate any benefit to be realized. Therefore, 2FA needs to be implemented in phased in approach, giving your employees time to get used to a different way of authentication.

But probably the biggest disadvantage of 2FA is that once again with the technological advancements that are taking place today, it is now quite probable that the Cyberattacker can break through now both lines of defense. This gives rise to the need of what is known as "Multifactor Authentication", or MFA for short.

MULTIFACTOR AUTHENTICATION

As the name suggests, MFA uses more than two authentication mechanisms to confirm the identity of an end user. It must make use of at least three, with even more as needed (in this regard, theoretically, there is no limit that can be placed on this). A technical definition of MFA is as follows:

> It is an authentication method that uses two or more distinct mechanisms to validate a user's identity, rather than relying on just a simple username and password combination. MFA helps prevent unauthorized access to applications and sensitive data, helping organizations defend against identity theft, cyberattacks, and data breaches.
>
> *(SOURCE: https://www.cyberark.com/what-is/mfa/)*

Although the definition above says two, in the real world, businesses implement at least three or more layers of security. The basic premise of MFA is almost the same as that of 2FA: If one line of defense is broken into, then the second line of defense becomes harder. But as stated in the last section, the Cyberattacker of today is now able to even break through this second line of defense.

So, the idea of MFA is that after a few unsuccessful attempts, the Cyberattacker will simply give up in frustration, or if they are still successful, the overall probability of he or she getting into something valuable (such as the digital assets) becomes significantly lower. So, if a company is hit with a security breach, they may install even more layers of security, in order to mitigate that particular risk from happening again in the future.

What are some of the benefits of using MFA? They are about the same as 2FA, but are different in some other areas. Here is a sample:

1) It can provide for limitless security:
   Since there is no required number of authentication mechanisms that you have to put into place, theoretically, your security posture could be at almost 100%. But of course in the real world, this is not really feasible.

2) Provides for more lines of defense:
   With 2FA, you are only given two layers of security. So, if the password were to be known, you are teetering on the edge of being broken into. But with MFA, since there is more than one layer of security, the statistical odds of this happening are greatly diminished.

3) It affords more customization:
   Although with 2FA you get some degree of flexibility of what you can use for authentication mechanisms, but with MFA, you have a much greater latitude in customizing your solution in order to meet not only the needs of your employees, but your overall security requirements as well.

4) It can work well with SSOs:
   These days, many wireless devices already come with an authentication mechanism that is embedded into them. A typical example of this are the newest brands of the iOS. They come with both Fingerprint Recognition ("TouchID") and Facial Recognition ("FaceID"). So, you can use one or the other to log into your iPhone. This is an example of a Single Sign Solution (SSO). If Apple decided to, it can even implement MFA with this SSO by simply deploying two or more differing authentication mechanisms into the iPhone.

5) Greater chances of compliance:
   Today, there is a plethora of data privacy laws; some of the more notable ones are the GDPR, CCPA, PCI-DSS, HIPAA, etc. Because these regulations have their own set of tenets and provisions, it can

be quite confusing for a CISO and their IT Security team to know what they need to compliance into. But by having MFA, you are actually increasing the odds that you will actually become compliant, even without you knowing about it.

6) <u>Enterprise mobility is now a reality</u>:

When COVID-19 hit, many companies in Corporate America were left scrambling to find security resolutions to issues that were never encountered before. Probably, the biggest example of this is the meshing of the home network with the corporate network, especially from the standpoint of authentication. But with MFA being deployed, this transition has now more or less been smoothened out. Now with work model being sort of a hybrid based one, proper and 100% authentication is now a must today.

7) <u>More applications for MFA</u>:

By starting out with a larger number of authentication mechanisms, you can now prune out more effectively which ones work and which ones not with your employees. Here you are taking a trial-and-use approach, rather than simply guessing with a 2FA approach. Although the role of MFA is to protect your shared resources at all costs, you also need to take the time and see which variation(s) of MFA work best with your employees. After all, they are the ones that will be using it the most, and it is also equally important that you have their buy in as well.

MFA, with its advantages, also comes with its setbacks, and in fact, they are the very same as those for the 2FA, but since there are more authentication mechanisms being used, you can magnify these cons probably to a much larger degree.

A simple MFA is illustrated below:

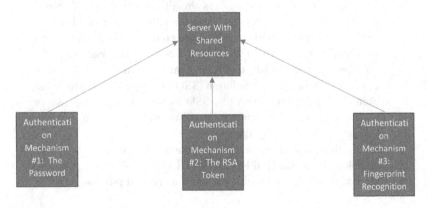

In the end, MFA is a far more robust choice to use than 2FA, because it addresses the three needs of authentication, which are as follows:

1) <u>Something you know</u>:
   This can be a password, or an answer to a challenge/response question.
2) <u>Something you have</u>:
   This can be an RSA token, a smart card, FOB, etc.
3) <u>Something you are</u>:
   This is typically your Biometrics, whether it is physical or behavioral based.

Technically, you can deploy either the 2FA or MFA into the Zero Trust Framework. Bur because constant verification is required, MFA has been the top choice so far by many companies who have deployed it. Also, with regard to authentication needs just outlined, it is Biometrics that seems to work the best, although there has been some pushback.

Therefore, the rest of this chapter is devoted to a review of Biometric Technology, with a primary focus on the following types of modalities:

1) <u>Fingerprint Recognition</u>:
   This is where the tip of your fingers is scanned.
2) <u>Iris Recognition</u>:
   This is where the unique features of your Iris are scanned.
3) <u>Facial Recognition</u>:
   This is where the unique features of your face are scanned.

Going forward in this book, whenever we discuss MFA, it will be these three above modalities that will comprise the three authentication mechanisms, as this is what will be used for the Zero Trust Framework, which will be explored in Chapter 5 of this book.

AN INTRODUCTION TO BIOMETRICS

Biometric Technology has actually been around for quite a long time, in fact, going back to the 1960s. This is when the first Hand Geometry Scanners came out, which was used primarily for Physical Access Entry applications. Instead of using a traditional lock and key approach to secure a door, all one had to do was wire this Hand Scanner to an electromagnetic lock strike. After the individual's identity was confirmed by the unique shape and structure of their hand, the lock strike would then unlock, and the door would open up automatically.

The next oldest modality to come out was that of Fingerprint Recognition. Mostly everybody has heard of this, because of its association with law enforcement on a global scale. It was during the height of 9/11 that Biometric Technology picked up a lot of interest. In this case, it was Facial Recognition which received the most attention. However, the technology was still in emerging stages at the time, and it did not live up to all of the hype that the media was giving it.

Once this happened, interest in Biometric Technology started to wane quickly, but then yet picked up momentum again once Cybersecurity started to catch fire. But this time, it was not looked as the primary means of defense, just given how expansive and complex Cybersecurity can be. Rather, it is now being looked at as an authentication mechanism in a 2FA or MFA role.

But before we move on any further, one may ask at this point, "Why has there always been such an interest in Biometrics?" Well, the truth of the matter is that it is one of the most reliable ways in which to confirm the identity of an individual with near 100% accuracy. The primary reason for this is that it is the unique characteristics of an individual that are being captured. Everybody has unique characteristics; thus, this is what makes Biometrics stand out in the world of Identity and Access Management (IAM).

DEFINITION AND UNIQUE FEATURES

Now that you have an idea of what Biometrics is about, a technical definition of it can be given as follows:

> A measurable physical characteristic or personal behavioral trait used to recognize the identity, or verify the claimed identity, of an applicant. Facial images, fingerprints, and iris scan samples are all examples of biometrics.
> *(SOURCE: https://csrc.nist.gov/glossary/term/biometrics)*

As this term has been used repeatedly in this chapter, the key thing here is to remember its uniqueness. We all have unique features, which separate us from everybody else in the world. The following matrix describes these features that can be used by a Biometric modality:

Biometric	Its Unique Features
The Fingerprint	The whorls, valleys, and ridges found on the Fingertip
The Face	The unique distances of the prominent features of the Face
The Iris	The unique orientations of objects that are found in the Iris
The Retina	The unique mapping of blood vessels that are found in the back of the eye, just ahead of the Optic Disc
The Voice	The unique inflections in our Voice when we speak
The Veins	The unique pattern of Veins found underneath the palm
The Keystroke	The unique typing pattern we have when typing on the keyboard
The Signature	This does not refer to the actual signature itself, but the unique mannerisms in which it is signed

So, as you can see from this matrix, there are two general categories of Biometrics:

1) The Physical Biometrics:
   This is where a biological sample is taken from an individual.
2) The Behavioral Biometrics:
   This is where a behavioral sample is taken from the individual.

THE PROCESS OF IDENTIFICATION

Although Biometrics may sound like a complex piece of technology, it really is not. In an ideal and optimal situation, a person can be identified in just 2 seconds or even less, depending on how recent or old the technology that is being used. Although there is quite a bit that happens behind the scenes during the identification process using Biometric Technology, the following will give a summary of how it actually happens, and it should be enough of a background once we embark on the chapter that reviews the Zero Trust Framework.

1) The Enrollment Process:
   In this scenario, a raw image is captured of the physiological (or behavioral) of an individual. A series of images are captured by the camera of the Biometric device, and compiled into one master

image. From here, the unique features are extracted, and stored permanently into the database of the Biometric database. This becomes technically the "Enrollment Template". This is illustrated below:

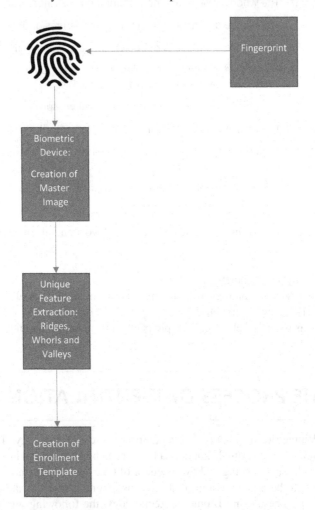

2) The Verification Process:

This is the step where the actual identification happens. But first, the end user must present their fingertip once again to the Biometric device. The same process occurs as in the Enrollment Process.

A brand new template is now created, and this is called the Verification Template. But this time, the Verification Template is not stored, but instead is compared with the Enrollment Template. If there is a close enough match (or a statistical correlation), then the end user is granted authorization to the shared resources that he or she is trying to access. This is illustrated below:

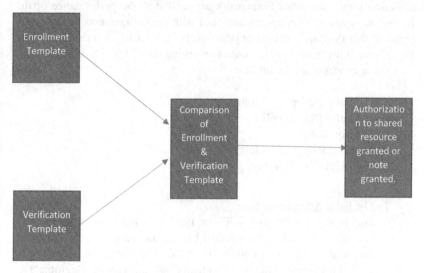

It should be noted that both the Enrollment and Verification templates are not the actual raw images of the fingertip. Rather, it is a mathematical representation of them, and in the case of this example, where Fingerprint Recognition is being used, it is a Binary Mathematical File, consisting of a nothing but a series of zeroes and ones like this:

**1010
1010**

So, the question gets asked: "What if a Cyberattacker steals my templates?" Well really, there is nothing to worry about. What can they do with it? Absolutely nothing. It's not like the same as Credit Card theft.

OTHER IMPORTANT CONCEPTS

When it comes to the other, relevant concepts of Biometrics, there are plenty of them, but they remain out of the context of this book. But the ones that are relevant to the Zero Trust Framework are related to the performance of the Biometric systems. They specifically deal with the optimization of these systems, so that they are working at peak levels in order to keep the Zero Trust Framework infrastructure of a company working on a 24 X 7 X 365 basis.

These concepts are as follows:

- The False Acceptance Rate
- The False Rejection Rate
- The Equal Rate
- The ability to verify rate
- The failure to enroll rate

1) The False Acceptance Rate:
   This is also known as "FAR", or Type II Errors. This is when an impostor is falsely authenticated by the Biometric system. In the case of the ZTF, this would be the chance that one of the Biometric modalities would actually authenticate and authorize an illegitimate end user into the shared resources server.

2) The False Rejection Rate:
   This is also known as the "FRR", or Type I Errors. This is when a legitimate end user is actually denied access to the shared resources, for whatever reason. For example, there could be a glitch in the Biometric device, or an effective physiological or behavioral set of images was not captured from the end user.

3) The Equal Error Rate:
   This is also known as the "ERR". This is where the False Acceptance Rate (FAR) and the False Rejection Rate (FRR) equal each other out. Actually, this is the optimal point for a Biometric device (or even system) to be at. This is illustrated below:

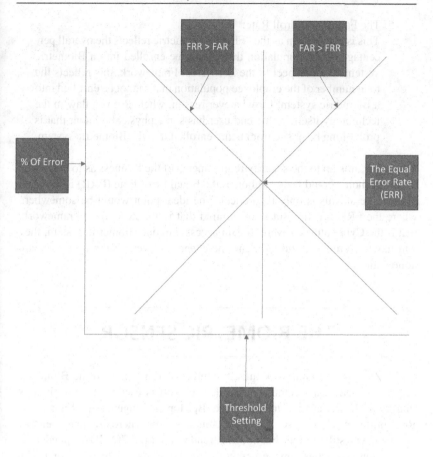

4) <u>The Ability To Verify Rate</u>:

This is also known as the "AVR", and this metric reflects the total percentage of the end user base that can be legitimately enrolled into a Biometric modality. With the Zero Trust Framework, this is the total number of employees that can be legitimately enrolled into all of the three Biometric modalities, and even more if necessary.

Mathematically, this can be represented as follows:

$$AVR = \left[(1 - FER) * (1 - FRR) \right]$$

5) <u>The Failure to Enroll Rate</u>:
This is also known as the "FER". This metric reflects the overall percentage of the population that cannot be enrolled into a Biometric system. With respect to the Zero Trust Framework, this reflects the total number of the employee population that cannot be enrolled into a Biometric system, for whatever reason, whether it is a flaw in the technology itself, or the end user has some physical ailment that is prohibiting he or she from being enrolled into the Biometric system.

Ultimately, it is up to the security requirements of the business as to where the ideal threshold should be at. Although the Equal Error Rate (ERR) is the ideal place to be at, this is only theoretical. The ideal point would be somewhere where the FRR > FAR. But keep in mind that in the Zero Trust Framework, that if the Cyber attacker were to gain access into one Biometric system, they still have two more to through, and the chances of getting through those are almost nil.

THE BIOMETRIC SENSOR

In the Zero Trust Framework infrastructure, when it comes to the Biometric devices themselves, a camera in the device itself is used to capture the raw images of the fingerprint, iris, and face. But for the longest time, Fingerprint Recognition has made use of a direct contact sensor. There are many vendors out there who still use this, but now the trend is, after the COVID-19 pandemic, to use non contactless image capture technology, like in the case of Facial Recognition and Iris Recognition.

Fingerprint Recognition devices have typically used what are known as "Optical Sensors". In this kind of set up, the end user places their fingertip on top of a platen. It is usually made from a glass composite and just underneath the platen, a Light Emitting Diode (LED) a light is flashed towards the optical sensor and is magnified by using a Charged Couple Device (CCD). It is essentially a camera that can transform any light pattern into a series of electrons.

Now, as the fingertip is placed onto the platen, the light (as just described) captures the ridges of the fingerprint back into the CCD. The ridges (from where a bulk of the unique features is captured from) appear as solid, dark lines.

Another alternative to the Optical Sensor is what is known as the Solid State sensor. But, rather than using a CCD, they use electrode arrays to capture the image of the ridges of the fingerprint. To get the raw images of the fingertip, a capacitance level is formed between the fingertip and the electrode. There are two types of Solid State sensors:

1) Many electrodes in which the entire image of the fingertip can be captured.
2) Fewer electrodes which used a sweeping mechanism, to capture the full image of the fingertip, by going left to right or right to left.

With regard to the non-contactless technology (as mentioned before), there are three kinds of sensors:

1) Reflection based:
   A light is shone onto the fingertip from different angles, using just one kind of camera.
2) Transmission based:
   A specialized red light is shined through the fingertip. Then, this light is aimed towards the sides of the fingertip.
3) Three-dimensional:
   Two different types of 3D scanning can be used:
   • Parametric Modeling: The images of the fingerprint are projected onto a cylindrical model and then from there, then onto a 2D print.
   • Non Parametric Modeling: Various mathematical algorithms are used to model the ridges of the fingertip, and are thus powerful enough to take into account any irregularities of the fingertip.

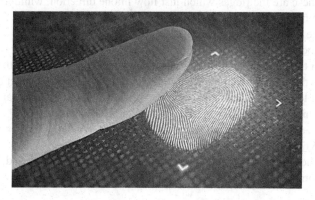

So as you can see, sensor technology, albeit a small component in the grand scheme of things, still plays a critical role in keeping the Zero Trust Framework infrastructure humming along. Any hiccups here can have still a huge impact.

Now that we have gone over some of the major principles of Biometrics in general, the rest of the chapter is devoted to reviewing in more detail the following Biometric modalities, which will be used in the Zero Trust Framework:

- Fingerprint Recognition
- Iris Recognition
- Facial Recognition

A REVIEW OF FINGERPRINT RECOGNITION

The raw images of the fingerprint are broken down into three distinct levels:

1) Level 1: The pattern images which are present in the fingerprint;
2) Level 2: The minutiae points of the fingerprint (this is from where a bulk of the unique features are actually extracted from);
3) Level 3: This includes the shapes and the images of the ridges, and its associated pores.

The ridges (as stated in this chapter) are a prime source for unique feature extraction. But there are other features as well, and they include the following:

1) Arches:
   These are the ridges which just flow in one direction, without doubling back, or going backwards. These only comprise about 5% of the features of the fingerprint;
2) Loops:
   In this feature, the ridges go backwards, and go from either the left to the right or from the right to the left. There are two distinct types of loops: a) Radial loops which go downward; and b) the ulnar loop which goes upwards on the fingerprint. These make up 65% of the features within the fingerprint;
3) Whorls:
   The ridges in the fingerprint make a circle around a core, and these comprise 30% of the features in the fingerprint.

In addition to the above features which are collected by a fingerprint recognition system, the actual number of ridges, and the way that these ridges are positioned (specifically their orientation) can also prove to be a very distinctive feature as well, and can help to contribute to the verification and/or identification of an individual.

The Process of Fingerprint Recognition

Fingerprint recognition follows a distinct methodology, which can be broken down into the following steps:

1) Raw Data Acquisition:
   The actual, raw images of the fingerprint are acquired through the sensor technology, which is being utilized. This means that the raw images which are collected are eventually examined by the biometric system to see if there is too much extraneous data in the fingerprint image, which could interfere in the acquisition of unique data. If there is too much of an obstruction found, the fingerprint device will automatically discard that particular image, and prompt the end user to place their finger into the platen for another raw image of the fingerprint to be collected. If the raw images are accepted, they are subsequently sent over to the processing unit, which is located within the fingerprint recognition device.

2) Unique feature extraction:
   With the raw images which have now been accepted by the system, the unique features are then extracted, and then stored as the enrollment template. If fingerprint recognition is being used by a smartphone, a smart card is then utilized to store the actual enrollment template, and can even provide for some processing features for the smartphone;

3) Authentication and Authorization:
   If the enrollment and verification templates are deemed to be close in similarity, the end user is then verified and/or identified, and is then granted physical or logical access to which they are seeking.

Fingerprint Recognition Quality Control Checks

The need to collect high-quality, raw images for the first time is of paramount importance for the Zero Trust Framework. The following are the quality control checks for fingerprint recognition:

1) Resolution:
   This refers to the total number of dots per inch (DPI), or also known as the total pixels per inch (PPI). Most fingerprint algorithms require a DPI or PPI resolutions of at least 250 to 300 DPI.

2) Area:
   This is the actual size of the scanned and captured fingerprint image. You need to have a minimum scanned fingerprint area of at least one

square inch. Anything less than that will not produce a good quality raw image.

3) <u>Frames Per Second</u>:

This is the total number of raw images the fingerprint recognition device sends to the processing unit. Of course, the higher number of frames per second means a much greater tolerance for any unwanted movements of the fingerprint on the platen.

4) <u>The Number of Fingerprint Pixels</u>:

This refers to the total number of pixels in the scanned image.

5) <u>The Dynamic Range</u>:

This refers to the possible ranges which are available for the encoding of each pixel value; at least eight bits is optimal.

6) <u>Geometric Accuracy</u>:

These are the geometric differences between the enrollment and the verification templates, and this is calculated via the deviations from the X and Y axes on the fingerprint template.

7) <u>The Image Quality</u>:

This is the variable which refers to the indentifying, unique features in the fingerprint, such as the ridgeline patterns and the various minutiae, which are extracted.

The second modality in line for the MFA component of the Zero Trust Framework is that of Facial Recognition, and is reviewed in the next section.

A REVIEW OF FACIAL RECOGNITION

Facial recognition technology relies upon the physical features of the face (see Figure 5), which are determined by genetics. Also, this technology can either be deployed as a fully automated system or as a semi-automated system. With the latter, no human interaction is needed, and all of the verification and identification decisions are made by the technology itself. With the latter, human intervention to a certain degree is required, and this is actually the preferred method for deploying a facial recognition system.

The unique features that are captured include the following:

1) The ridges between the eyebrows;
2) The cheekbones;
3) The mouth edges;
4) The distances between the eyes;

5) The width of the nose;
6) The contour and the profile of the jawline;
7) The chin.

To start the process of raw image collection, the individual must first either stand before a camera, or unknowingly, have their face captured with covert surveillance methods, such as using a CCTV camera system (with the technology that is available today, facial recognition can literally be implanted in a CCTV).

Once the raw images are collected by the camera, the data is then either aligned or normalized to help refine the raw images at much more granular level. The refinement techniques involved include adjusting the face to be in the middle of the pictures which have been taken, and adjusting the size and the angle of the face so that the best unique features can be extracted and later converted over to the appropriate verification and enrollment templates.

All of this is done via mathematical algorithms. As mentioned previously, facial recognition is countered by a number of major obstacles, but even more so at the raw image acquisition phase. These include a lack of subtle differentiation between the faces and other obstructive variables in the external environment, various different facial expressions and poses in subsequent raw image captures, and capturing a landmark orienting feature such as the eyes.

The Techniques of Facial Recognition – Unique Feature Extraction

There are two techniques that are involved with Facial Recognition, which are as follows:

1) Appearance based;
2) Model based.

With appearance-based facial recognition techniques, a face can be represented in several object views, and it is based on one image only, and no three-dimensional models are even utilized. The specific methodologies here include Principal Component Analysis and Linear Discriminant Analysis. Model-based facial recognition techniques construct and create a three-dimensional model of the human face, and after that point onwards, the facial variations can be captured and computed. The specific methodology here includes Elastic Bunch Graph Mapping. All of these techniques will now be discussed in greater detail.

With Principal Component Analysis (this is linear based, also known as PCA), this technique dates all the way back to 1988, when it was first used for facial recognition. This technique primarily uses what is known as "Eigenfaces". Simply put, Eigenfaces are just merely two-dimensional spectral facial images, which are composed of grayscale features.

There are literally hundreds of Eigenfaces, which can be stored in the database of a facial recognition system. When facial images are collected by the system, this library of Eigenfaces is placed over the raw images that are superimposed over one another. At this point, the level of variances between the Eigenfaces and the raw images are then subsequently computed, averaged together, and then different weights are assigned.

The end result is a one-dimensional image of the face, which is then processed by the facial recognition system. In terms of mathematics, PCA is merely a linear transformation in which the facial raw images get converted over into a geometrical coordinate system. Imagine if you will, a quadrant-based system. With the PCA technique, the data set with the greatest variance lies upon the first coordinate of the quadrant system (this is also termed the first Principal Component Analysis), the next data set with the second largest variance falls onto the second coordinate, and so on, until the one-dimensional face is created.

The biggest disadvantages with this technique are that it requires a full frontal image, and as a result, a full image of the face is required. Thus, any changes in any facial feature require a full recalculation of the entire Eigenface process. However, a refined approach has been developed, thus greatly reducing the calculating and processing time which is required.

With Linear Discriminant Analysis (this is linear based, also known as LDA), the aim is to project the face onto a vector space, with the primary objective being to speed up the verification and identification processes by cutting down drastically on the total number of features which need to be matched.

The mathematics behind LDA is to calculate the variations which occur between a single raw data point from a single raw data record. Based from these calculations, the linear relationships are then extrapolated and formulated. One of the advantages of the LDA technique is that it can actually take into account the lighting differences and the various types of facial expressions which can occur, but still, a full face image is required.

After the linear relationship is drawn from the variance calculations, the pixel values are captured, and statistically plotted. The resultant is a computed raw image, which is just simply a linear relationship of the various pixel values. This raw image is called a Fisher Face, which can be seen in. Despite the advantages, a major drawback of the LDA technique is that it does require a large database.

With the Elastic Bunch Graph Matching (this is model based, also known as EBGM) technique, this looks at the nonlinear mathematical relationships of the face, which includes factors such as lighting differences, and the differences in the facial poses and expressions. This technique uses a similar technique, which is used in iris recognition, known as Gabor Wavelet Mathematics.

With the EBGM technique, a facial map is created, and an example of this can be seen. The facial image on the map is just a sequencing of graphs, with various nodes located at the landmark features of the face, which include the eyes, edges of the lips, tips of the nose, etc. These edge features become two-dimensional distance vectors, and during the identification and verification processes, various Gabor mathematical filters are used to measure and calculate the variances of each node on the facial image.

Then, Gabor mathematical wavelets are used to capture up to five spatial frequencies, and up to eight different facial orientations. Although the EBGM technique does not at all require a full facial image, the main drawback with this technique is that the landmarks of the facial map must be marked extremely accurately, with great precision.

The next section now looks at the third Biometric modality to be used in the Zero Trust Framework; this is Iris Recognition. This is what will give the MFA its very powerful features, because Iris Recognition is deemed to be the most powerful modality of all, given its deep and unique features.

IRIS RECOGNITION

Iris recognition has developed so quickly that now images of the iris can be captured at much greater distances, as well as when people are in movement. Previously, an end user had to stand directly in front of the iris recognition camera, at a very close proximity. And now, even the unique pattern of the blood vessels can also be scanned, and this will be examined after the section on retinal recognition.

The Physiological Structure of the Iris

The iris lies between the pupil and the white of the eye, which is known as the sclera. The color of the iris varies from individual to individual, but there is a commonality to the colors, and these include green, blue, brown, and in remote cases, even a hazel color can occur. And in even in the most extreme cases, a combination of these colors can be seen in the iris. The color of the iris is primarily determined by the DNA code inherited from our parents.

The unique patterns of the iris start to form when the human embryo is conceived; usually, this happens during the third month of fetal gestation. The phenotype of the iris is shaped and formed in a process known as chaotic morphogenesis, and the unique structures of the iris are completely formed during the first two years of child development.

The primary purpose of the iris is to control the diameter and the size of the pupil. The pupil is that part of the eye, located in the back of the eye, which allows for light to enter into the eye and in turn reaches the retina. Of course, the amount of light which can enter the pupil is a direct function of how much it can expand and contract, which is governed by the muscles of the iris. The iris is primarily composed of two layers: (1) A fibrovascular tissue known as the stroma, and (2) The stroma is in turn connected to a grouping of muscles known as the sphincter muscles.

It is this muscle which is responsible for the contraction of the pupil, and another group of muscles known as the dilator muscles govern the expansion of the pupil. When you look at your iris in the mirror, you will notice a radiating pattern. This pattern is known as the trabecular meshwork. When Near Infrared Light (NIR) is flashed onto the iris, many unique features can be observed. These features include ridges, folds, freckles, furrows, arches, crypts, coronas, as well as other patterns, which appear in various discernable fashions.

Finally, the collaretta of the iris is the thickest region of it, which gives the iris its two distinct regions, known as the pupillary zone (this forms the boundary of the pupil), and the ciliary zone (which fills up the rest of the iris). Other unique features can also be seen in the collaretta region. The iris is deemed to be one of the most unique structures of human physiology, and in fact, each individual has a different iris structure in both eyes. In fact, even scientific studies have shown that identical twins have different iris structures.

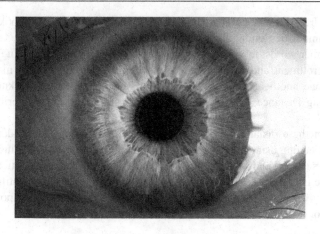

Iris Recognition: How It Works

The idea of using the iris to confirm the identity of an individual dates all the way back to 1936, when an ophthalomologist by the Frank Burch first proposed the idea. This idea was then patented in 1987 and by the mid-nineties; Dr. John Daugmann of the University of Cambridge developed the first mathematical algorithms for it. Traditional iris recognition technology requires that the end user stands no more than 10 inches away from the camera.

With the NIR light shined into the iris, various grayscale images are then captured, and then compiled into one primary composite photograph. Special software then removes any obstructions from the iris, which can include portions of the pupil, eyelashes, eyelids, and any resulting glare from the iris camera.

From this composite image, the unique features of the iris (as described before) are then "zoned off" into hundreds of phasors (also known as vectors), whose measurements and amplitude level are then extracted (using Gabor Wavelet mathematics), and then subsequently converted into a binary mathematical file, which is not greater than 500 bytes. Because of this very small template size, verification of an individual can occur in just less than one second.

From within the traditional iris recognition methods, this mathematical file then becomes the actual iris biometric template, which is also known as the "IrisCode". However, in order to positively verify or identify an individual from the database, these iris-based enrollment and verification templates (the IrisCode) must be first compared with one another. In order to accomplish this task, the IrisCodes are compared against one another byte by byte, looking for any dissimilarities among the string of binary digits.

In other words, to what percentage do the zeroes and the ones in the iris-based enrollment and verification templates match up and do not match up against one another? This answer is found by using a technique known as "Hamming Distances", which is even used in iris recognition algorithms of today.

After these distances are measured, tests of statistical independence are then carried out, using high-level Boolean mathematics (such as Exclusive OR Operators [XOR] and Masked Operators). Finally, if the test of statistical independence is passed, the individual is then positively verified or identified, but if the tests of statistical independence failed, then the person is **NOT** positively verified or identified.

CONCLUSIONS

Overall, this chapter has examined some of the major components that make up the Zero Trust Framework:

1) Two-Factor Authentication (2FA);
2) Multifactor Authentication (MFA);
3) Biometric Technology.

Going forward into the rest of this book, only MFA will be considered for the Zero Trust Framework, which will be examined in more detail in Chapter 4 of this book. In the author's view, the use of 2FA will soon be outnumbered, as the Cyberattacker is now well prepared to break into two lines of defense, and perhaps even more. This is why MFA is so important.

With the extra layers of defense that it does present, it lessens the statistical odds that a Cyberattacker will break through all of the lines of authentication. In theory, this is possible with the other types of authentication mechanisms, but so far, this has not proven to be the case with Biometric Technology. The primary reason for this is that it is almost close to impossible, if not difficult to replicate somebody's fingerprint, and especially the iris.

There are still some doubts about the face, but the reason it was included is that it provides for a still very valuable line of defense, and that it is as contactless as well, given the society that we live in today. Also, the other Biometric Technologies (as they were examined earlier in this chapter) still have some ways to go in terms of commercial adoption, thus they would not be a good choice for a Zero Trust Framework.

Also going forward into the rest of the book, the order of arrangement for the Biometric modalities in terms of authentication will be as follows: Fingerprint Recognition, Iris Recognition. This is illustrated in the diagram below:

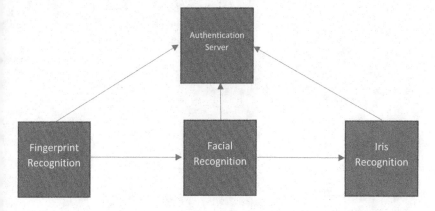

The next chapter of this book will do a greater examination of what is known as "BioCryptography". This is when the principles of Cryptography are used to further protect the Biometric Templates.

The Public Key Infrastructure and BioCryptography

3

Our last chapter reviewed some of the fundamental components that belong to the Zero Trust Framework (ZTF). It reviewed in detail the concepts of 2FA, MFA, and the Biometric Technologies that are to be used in any kind of Zero Trust deployment. In the end, it was concluded that MFA and the use of Biometrics as the authentication mechanisms would prove to be of most value and importance to a ZTF.

In the examples that we provided in the last chapter, they all shared one common denominator: It was assumed that there was only one user accessing one shared resource. In terms of mathematics, this can be represented as a one to one, or 1: 1 relationship. But in the real world, ZTF deployments will not be this direct. Rather, they will be more complex in nature, and utilize an approach in which there will be many employees accessing many different types and kinds of shared resources, possibly even across different servers that are physically located apart from one another.

Thus, in this case, you want a ZTF which will take the form of what is known as an "Asymmetric Key Cryptography" approach. This is where both public and private keys are used to further protect the Biometric Templates as they are in transit from the point of authentication to the point authorization. As it was mentioned in the previous chapter, Biometric Templates are quite strong in nature.

They are nothing but mathematical representations of our unique physiological and/or behavioral traits. In the end, if the Cyberattacker were to break through a database and hijack them, there is hardly anything much that they can do with them. As pointed before, it is not the like the same thing as credit card theft, where a hacker can literally run "amuck" with it, and make all kinds of fraudulent purchases with it.

But the fact that a Cyberattacker can even entertain the thoughts of heisting these Biometric Templates, which are so crucial to a ZTF, means that there is an inherent weakness in the framework that needs to be remediated, and this can only be done by using the principles of Cryptography. Thus, it is the Asymmetric Key approach, which can provide the best protection for these Biometric Templates. This methodology is also referred to as the "Public Key Infrastructure", or "PKI" for short, and this referencing will be used throughout the remainder of this book.

In this chapter, we will lay down the foundations for the PKI, which will be the model used to support our ZTF model in Chapter 5. After we introduce the concepts of what it takes to protect these Biometric Templates, the next point of issue that will be dealt with is how to ensure the integrity of these Biometric Templates remain intact from the point of authorization to the point of authentication, as they will be reused over constantly in order to grant access to the shared resources the end user is trying to gain access to.

The ultimate goal here is once the employee has been enrolled into all three Biometric modalities, they will never have to do it again, unless of course something catastrophic happens, such as a natural disaster or security breaching occurring. Therefore, it is of paramount importance to make sure that the Biometric Templates remain the same all of the time, without any alterations being made for them. There is one solution for this, and that is making use of Hashing Algorithms, which will be covered at the end of this chapter.

Also, this will give rise to the need for Privileged Access Management, or PAM, to make sure that all of the access accounts of the employees remain secure and are assigned properly, since the intention is to avoid having to go through the authentication process repeatedly (and only once). This is a concept that will be further explored in Chapter 5 of this book.

AN OVERVIEW OF THE PUBLIC KEY INFRASTRUCTURE (PKI)

A PKI can be a very large undertaking, or even just a smaller one, depending upon the size and the requirements of the company in question. But generally speaking, setting up a PKI takes more time than it does using a

Symmetric Key Cryptography approach. This kind of approach would be ideal to use in the examples that we have provided so far in this book, as we have assumed thus far that it has been just one employee trying to access one shared resource.

But, you do not see this approach being used in the real world, because of the many security risks that it can pose. Therefore, the use of the PKI remains to be the viable choice. In the rest of this chapter, we will introduce the important concepts of the PKI. We will then move onto the topic of BioCryptography, which is the science of using Cryptography to protect Biometric Templates. Finally, we will then delve into the topic of Hashing Algorithms.

WHAT IT IS ALL ABOUT

In the world of PKI, there are two primary keys that are used, and they are called the public and the private key, and are also used to encrypt and decrypt the plaintext, which is sent between the sending and the receiving parties as they communicate with another. In the most simplistic terms, a PKI can be likened to that of a safety box at a local bank. In this example, normally, there are two sets of keys, which are used.

One key is the one which the back gives to you. This can be referred to as the public key, because it is used over and over again by past renters of this particular safety deposit box, and for other, future renters as well. The second key is the private key, which the bank keeps in their possession at all times, and only the bank personnel know where it is kept.

A PKI is just like this example, but of course, it is much more complex than this in practice. To start off with, typically, it is the receiving party which is primarily responsible for generating both the public and the private key. In this situation, let us refer to the public key as "pk", and the private key as "sk".

So, to represent both of these keys together, it would be mathematically represented as (pk,sk). It is then the sending party which uses the public key (pk) to encrypt the message they wish to send to the receiving party, which then uses the private key (sk), which they have privately and personally formulated to decrypt the encrypted ciphertext from the sending party.

One of the primary goals of a PKI is to avoid the need for both the sending and the receiving parties from having to meet literally face to face in order to decide on how to protect (or encrypt) their communications with another. So, at this point, the question then arises is, how does the sending party know about the public key (pk) generated by the receiving party so that the two can communicate with each other?

The Public Key and the Private Key

There are two distinct ways in which this can be accomplished:

1) The receiving party can deliberately and purposefully notify the sending party of the public key (pk) in a public channel, so that communications can be initiated;
2) The sending party and the receiving party do not know anything about each other in advance. In this case, the receiving party makes their public key known on a global basis so that whoever wishes to communicate with the receiving party can do so, as a result.

Now, this brings up a very important point: The public key is literally "public", meaning that anybody can use it. So, how does a PKI remain secure? It remains solely on the privacy of the private key (sk), which is being utilized. In these cases, it is then up to the receiving party now to share the private key (sk) with any other party, no matter how much they are trusted.

If the privacy of the secret key (sk) is compromised in any way, then the security scheme of a PKI is totally compromised. In order to help ensure that the private keys remain private, the PKI uses the power of prime numbers (also known as the "RSA algorithm"). The basic idea here is to create a very large prime number as a product of multiplying two very large prime numbers together.

Mathematically put, the basic premise is that it will take a hacker a very long time to figure out the two prime number multiples of a very large product which is several hundred integers long, and thus, give up in frustration. Even if a hacker were to spend the time to figure out one of these prime numbers, the hacker still has to figure out the other prime number, and the chances that they will figure this out is almost nil.

As a result, only one portion of the (pk, sk) is figured out, and the PKI still remains intact and secure. In other words, the hacker cannot reverse engineer one key to get to the other key to break the ciphertext. It should also be noted that in the PKI, the same public key can be used by multiple, different sending parties to communicate with the single receiving party, thus forming a one to many, or 1:N mathematical relationship.

This is illustrated in the diagram below:

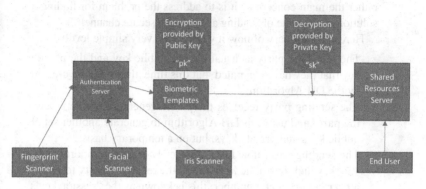

The Mathematical Algorithms of the PKI

There are number of key mathematical algorithms which serve as the crux for PKI. They are as follows:

1) The RSA Algorithm:

   In terms of the RSA Algorithm, this is probably the most famous and widely used PKI cryptography algorithm. In fact, this very algorithm will serve as the foundation for BioCryptography later in this chapter. The RSA Algorithm originates from the RSA Data Security Corporation, and is named after the inventors who created it, which are Ron Rivest, Adi Shamir, and Leonard Adelman.

   As it was just reviewed previously, the RSA Algorithm uses the power of prime numbers to create both the public key and the private key. But, using large keys to encrypt such large amounts of data is totally infeasible, from the standpoint of the processing power and central server resources. Instead ironically, the encryption is done as symmetric algorithms (such as the ones reviewed previously), and then the private key gets further encrypted by the receiving party's public key.

   Once the receiving party obtains their ciphertext from the sending party, then the private key generated by the symmetric cryptography algorithm is decrypted, and public key which was generated by asymmetric cryptography can then be subsequently used to decrypt the rest of the ciphertext.

2) The Diffie-Hellman Algorithm:

   In terms of the Diffie Hellman asymmetric algorithm, it is named after its inventors as well, who are Whit Diffie and Martin Hellman. It is also known as the DH algorithm for short as well. But interestingly enough, this algorithm is not used for the encryption of the ciphertext, rather the main concern of it is to address the problem for finding a solution of the issue of sending a key over a secure channel.

Here is a summary of how it works, on a very simple level:

- The receiving party as usual has the public key and the private key that they have generated, but this time, they both are created by the DH Algorithm;
- The sending party receives the public generated by the receiving party and uses this DH Algorithm to generate another set of public keys and private keys, but on a temporary basis;
- The sending party now takes this newly created temporary private key and the public key sent by the receiving party to generate a random, secret number; this is known as the "session key";
- The sending party uses this newly established session key to encrypt the ciphertext message, and sends this forward to the receiving party, with the public key that they have temporarily generated;
- When the receiving party finally receives the ciphertext from the sending party, the session key can now be derived mathematically;
- Once the above step has been completed, the receiving party can now decrypt the rest of the ciphertext.

3) The Elliptical Wave Theory Algorithm:

Finally, with Elliptical Wave Theory, it is a much newer type of PKI mathematical algorithm. It can be used to encrypt very large amounts of data, and its main advantage is that it is very quick, and does not require a lot of server overhead or processing time. As its name implies, Elliptical Wave Theory first starts with a parabolic curve drawn on a normal x,y coordinate Caretesian plane.

After the first series of X and Y coordinates are plotted, various lines are then drawn through the image of the curve, and this process continues until many more curves are created and their corresponding, intersecting lines are also created.

Once this process has been completed, the plotted X and Y coordinates of each of the intersected lines and parabolic curves are then extracted. Once this extraction has been completed, then all of the hundreds and hundreds of X and Y coordinates are then added together in order to create the public and the private key. But, the trick to decrypting a ciphertext message encrypted by Elliptical Wave Theory is that the receiving party has to know the shape of the original elliptical curve, and all of the X and Y coordinates of the lines where they intersect with the various curves, and the actual starting point at which the addition of the X and Y coordinates first started.

The Components of the PKI

It should be noted at this point that the Public Keys and the Private Keys in a PKI are also referred to as "Digital Certificates". Thus, going forward in this book, that is how they will be referred to. The components of a PKI, and as it relates to the ZTF, are as follows:

1) The Certificate Authority, also known as the CA:
   This is the outside third party who issues the digital certificates.
2) The Digital Certificate:
   As mentioned, this consists of both the private key and the public key, which are issued by the CA. This is also the entity that the end user would go to in case he or she needed to have a digital certificate verified. These digital certificates are typically kept as the points of authentication and authorization, respectively.
3) The LDAP or X.500 Directories:
   These are the databases which collect and distribute the digital certificates from the CA.
4) The Registration Authority, also known as the RA:
   If the place of business or organization has a large ZTF (such as a multinational corporation), this entity then usually handles and processes the requests for the required digital certificates, and then transmits those requests to the CA to process and create the required digital certificates.

The CA can be viewed as the main governing body, or even the king of the PKI of the ZTF. In order to start using the Public Key Infrastructure to communicate with others, it is the Certificate Authority which issues the digital certificates, which once again, consists of both the public and private keys.

The Digital Certificates

Each digital certificate which is generated by the Certificate Authority consists of the following technical specifications:

1) The Digital Certificate Version Number:
   Typically, it is either version number 1, 2, or 3.
2) The Serial Number:
   This is the unique ID number which separates and distinguishes a particular Digital Certificate from all of the others (this can be likened to each Digital Certificate having its own Social Security Number).

3) The Signature Algorithm Identifier:
This contains the information and data about the mathematical algorithm used by the Certificate Authority to issue the particular Digital Certificate.

4) The Issuer Name:
This is the actual name of the Certificate Authority which is issuing the Digital Certificate to the place of business or organization.

5) The Validity Period:
This contains both the activation and deactivation dates of the Digital Certificates; in other words, this is the lifetime of the Digital Certificate as determined by the Certificate Authority.

6) The Public Key:
This is created by the Certificate Authority.

7) The Subject Distinguished Name:
This is the name which specifies the Digital Certificate owner.

8) The Subject Alternate Name Email:
This specifies the Digital Certificate's owner Email address (this is where the actual Digital Certificates go to).

9) The Subject Name URL:
This is the Web Address of the place of business or organization to whom the Digital Certificates are issued to.

How Public Key Infrastructure Works

Below is a description of how the PKI would work for a ZTF:

1) The request for the Digital Certificate is sent to the appropriate Certificate Authority;

2) After this request has been processed, the Digital Certificate is issued to the person who is requesting it;

3) The Digital Certificate then gets signed by confirming the actual identity of the person who is requesting that particular Digital Certificate;

4) The Digital Certificate can now be used to encrypt the plaintext into the ciphertext, which is sent from the sending party to the receiving party.

The Registration Authority is also known as the RA, as eluded to before. The RA is merely a subset of the CA, or rather, it is not intended to replace or take over the role of the CA; instead, it is designed to help if it becomes overwhelmed with digital certificate request traffic.

However, the RA by itself does not grant any type or kind of digital certificates, nor does it confirm the identity of the person who is requesting the digital certificate. Rather, its role is to help process the requests until the processing queue at the CA becomes much more manageable.

The RA sends all of the digital certificate requests in one big batch, rather than one at a time. This process is known as "chaining certificates". The RA is typically found in very large, multinational corporations, where each office location would have its own RA, and the CA would reside at the main, corporate headquarters.

Finally, all digital certificate requests are processed by the RA, which are also associated with a chain of custody trail, for security auditing purposes. The RA can be viewed as a support vehicle for the CA, in which a mathematical, hierarchal relationship exists.

Public Key Infrastructure Policies and Rules

It should be noted at this point that in order for either the Certificate Authority or the Registration Authority to function properly in a ZTF, it is important to have a distinct set of rules and policies in place. These surround the use of the issuance, storage, and the revocation of the expired digital certificate. While it is out of the scope of this book to get into the exact details of all these rules and policies, the following is just a sampling of some of the topics which need to be addressed:

1) Where and how the records and the audit logs of the Certificate Authority are to be kept, stored, and archived;
2) The administrative roles for the Certificate Authority;
3) Where and how the public keys and the private keys are to be kept, stored, and also backed up;
4) What is the length of time for which the public keys and the private keys will be stored;
5) If public or private key recovery will be allowed by the Certificate Authority;
6) The length of the time of the validity period for both the public keys and private keys;
7) What will be the technique in which the Certificate Authority can delegate the responsibilities to the Registration Authority;
8) Will the digital certificates to be issued by the Certificate Authority be used for applications and resources;
9) If the digital certificates to be issued by the Certificate Authority be used for the sole purposes of just encryption of the ciphertext;

10) If there are any types or kinds of applications which should be refused to have digital certificates;

11) When a digital certificate is initially authorized by the Certificate Authority, will there be a finite period of time when the digital certificate will be subject to revocation.

As one can see, based upon the establishment of the many rules and policies which need to be set into place, the actual deployment and establishment of a Public Key Infrastructure in a ZTF can become quite complex, depending upon the size and the need of the particular business or organization.

The LDAP Protocol

In terms of the database structure for the digital certificates, this is most useful and effective when the LDAP servers are utilized. LDAP is merely an acronym which stands for "Lightweight Directory Access Protocol", and is simply a database protocol which is used for the updating and searching of the directories which run over the TCP/IP network protocol (this is the network protocol which is primarily used by the PKI Infrastructure for the ZTF).

It is the job of the LDAP server of the Public Key Infrastructure to contain such information and data as it relates to the digital certificates, the public and the private key storage locations, as well as the matching public and private key labels.

The Certificate Authority uses a combination of the end user name and the matching tags to specifically locate the digital certificates on the LDAP server. From that point onwards, it is the LDAP server which then checks to see if the requested digital certificate is valid or not, and it if it is valid, it then retrieves from its database a digital certificate which can then be sent to the end user. Although all digital certificates which are issued have a finite lifespan when they are first issued, they can also be revoked for any reason at any time by the Public Key Infrastructure Administrator.

In order to accomplish this very specific task, a Certificate Revocation List, or a CRL is used. This list is composed of the digital certificate serial numbers which have been assigned by the Certificate Authority. But, looking at this type of information and data can be very taxing on the system resources and processes.

Therefore, in this regard, it is obviously much easier to reissue the digital certificates as they expire, rather than to revoke them and then having to reissue them again, and of course, which would mean that the Public Key Infrastructure System Administrator would then have to update the Certificate Revocation List.

The PKI Standards

The Public Key Infrastructure is also governed by a body known as the Public Key Cryptography Standards, also known as the PKCS. The bottom line here is that a smooth-running PKI will lead to an efficient and effective ZTF. The first of these standards has been previously described, and they are the RSA Encryption Standard, the Diffie-Hellman Key Agreement Standard, and the Elliptical Wave Theory. The other sets of standards which define a Public Key Infrastructure are as follows:

1) The Password-Based Cryptography Standard:
   This describes how to encrypt a private key with a secret key which is derived from a password.
2) The Extended Certificate Syntax Standard:
   This is merely a set of attributes attached onto a Digital Certificate which has been assigned by the Certificate Authority.
3) The Cryptographic Message Syntax Standard:
   This standard specifically outlines how to put the digital signatures into digital certificate envelopes, and from there, put that into another digital envelope.
4) The Private Key Information Syntax Standard:
   This standard directly specifies what kind of information and data should be included into a private key, and how that specific key should be formatted.
5) The Selected Attribute Types:
   This is a detailed list which at length describes the certain encryption attribute types for the last three standards.
6) The Certification Request Syntax Standard:
   This provides the details for the syntax for the digital certificates. Essentially, this standard simply sets forth the parameters which are needed for the Certificate Authority to understand the digital certificate request.
7) The Cryptographic Token Interface Standard:
   This is an Application Programming Interface (API) for specifying and handling the cryptographic functions as it relates to the smartcards.
8) The Personal Information Exchange Standard:
   This standard specifies exactly how an end user's private keys should be transported across the network medium.
9) The Cryptographic Token Information Format Standard:
   This standard specifies how the applications at a place of business or organization should interface with smart cards.

In the world of Public Key Infrastructure, it should be remembered that the public keys and the private keys (also known as the digital certificates) are created instantaneously and all of the time, whenever the need for access to shared resources is required. In fact, public keys and private keys are everywhere in a Public Key Infrastructure, even when one establishes a Secure Shell (SSH) connection over the Internet with their particular brand of web browser (this typically uses 128-Bit Encryption).

In fact, there are even public keys and private keys in the Public Key Infrastructure which are only used once, terminated, and are literally discarded away. These types of public keys and private keys are known more commonly as "session keys". In the end, digital certificates are nothing more than computer files.

Parameters of Public Keys and Private Keys

But before the actual public key or the private key can go out in the ZTF, it needs to have certain parameters which are specified to it, and these are as follows:

1) The type of mathematical algorithm which should be used;
2) How many bits of data the public keys and the private keys should be composed of;
3) The expiration date of both the public keys and the private keys.

Also, in order to keep the hackers at bay, it is equally important that not all of the public keys and the private keys are used all the time in the communication process between the sending and the receiving parties. It is also important to keep the public keys and the private keys fresh, or in other words, it is important to introduce randomness into the Public Key Infrastructure.

Such randomness is known as "Entropy", and this entropy is created by what is known as "Random Number Generators", and "Psuedo-Random Number Generators." Also, in a Public Key Infrastructure, there are different classes of both public keys and private keys. Here is a listing of just some of these classes of keys:

1) Signing Keys:
   These are the keys to create the digital signatures.
2) Authentication Keys:
   These are the keys which are created to authenticate computers, servers, and the receiving parties and the sending parties with one another.
3) Data Encryption Keys:
   These are the keys which are used to encrypt the files.

4) Session Keys:
These are the types of keys which are used to help secure a channel across an entire network for only a very short period of time.

5) Key Encryption Keys:
These types of keys literally wrap the ciphertext to provide further protection between the sending and the receiving parties.

6) Reof Key:
This is the master which is used for signing all of the other public keys and private keys which originate specifically from the Certificate Authority.

A REVIEW INTO BIOCRYPTOGRAPHY

Biocryptography provides the means to further biometric templates at these critical junctures. As it was reviewed in Chapter 2 of this book, Cryptography is the science of scrambling information and data which is transit across a network medium, and then descrambling it at the receiving end into a decipherable format.

That way, if the scrambled information and data were to be intercepted by a third party, there is not much which can be done unless they possess the keys for descrambling the information. These concepts of scrambling and descrambling can be very easily applied to Biometrics. This is formally known as "BioCryptography".

In other words, the Biometric Templates are protected by scrambling and descrambling keys while they are stored in the database or in movement across a network to the shared resources server.

To review, whenever we send a message to our intended recipient-whether it is by e-mail, instant message, or even just a text message on our Smartphone, this message is often sent as a "plaintext", or "cleartext".

This means that the actual message is being transmitted to the intended recipient in the way it was originally constructed by the originator of the message. Thus, the only true way to protect the information being sent is to scramble it, in other words, "encrypt the message". This encrypted (or now scrambled message) is now known as the "ciphertext".

The reverse of this process is known as "decryption", with the end result being a readable message to the intended recipient. As all of this relates to Biometrics, the data packet which houses the biometric template (such as the fingerprint or iris recognition template) can be viewed as the plain text, or as the "Plaintext Biometric Template".

The Cipher Biometric Template

When the fingerprint or iris template is encrypted, it can be viewed as the "Cipher Biometric Template", and when it is decrypted, it can be viewed once again as the decrypted "Plaintext Biometric Template". But other than just doing the above, Biocryptography also has to provide the following three functions in order for it to be truly effective:

1) Authentication:
   The shared resources server of the Plaintext Biometric Template) should be able to, 100%, verify the origin of it.
2) Integrity:
   The message in transit (or the Plaintext Biometric Template) should not be modified in any way or format while it is in transit (or in other words, replacing a fingerprint biometric template with an iris biometric template in order to spoof the biometric system).
3) Non-repudiation:
   The sender of the Plaintext Biometric Template should not falsely deny that they have not sent that particular template originally.

Biocryptography in an MFA for the Zero Trust Framework

Although this has been illustrated and reviewed to a certain extent in earlier parts of this book, we are now at a critical juncture where a detailed examination of how all of this comes together. First, as described, there are three main Biometric modalities that will constitute the MFA methodology for the ZFT. There is a logical flow sequence as to how the end user or employee will be authenticated in this process. The following illustration summarizes this:

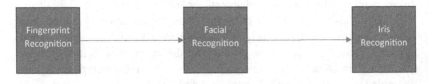

All of these devices will be wired to the authentication server. It is assumed that both the enrollment and verification process will happen in a rapid fire succession, in perhaps under just a two or minutes. Once this process has been done, all of the Verification Templates will then be scrambled and created to form as to what will be known as the "Cipher Biometric Template". This newly created template will then be further encased into another data packet, for an added measure of protection.

From here, this new template will then be transmitted over to the authentication server so that the end user (or employee) will be granted access to the shared resources that they are seeking to use. In this situation, there are two important points to remember:

1) The newly created Verification Template will actually be a combination of the Fingerprint, Facial, and Iris Recognition Verification Templates. This is what will be sent to the authentication server after this newly created template has been scrambled and encapsulated into another data packet.

2) One of the primary goals is that once the end user (or employee) has been authenticated once, they will not be required to go through this process again. Rather, it is the newly created Verification Template that will be used repeatedly to allow access to the shared resources server. This is where the concept of Privileged Access Management will come into play, and will be further reviewed in detail in Chapter 5 of this book. The ultimate goal here is to create what is known as "One Identity for Life", thus eradicating the use of the password all together.

The process for the newly created Verification Template is illustrated below:

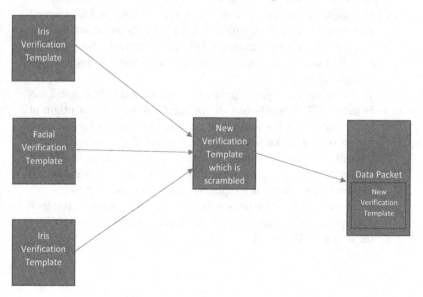

The assumption so far is that the end user (or employee) in this MFA approach for the ZTF is at the physical place of the business location. But given the work dynamics of today's environment, it is also important to address as to how this methodology will work for a remote employee, located hundreds, or perhaps even thousands of miles away.

BIOCRYPTOGRAPHY AND VIRTUAL PRIVATE NETWORKS

There is yet another tool of BioCryptography which would perfectly here for the Remote Employee – this is known as a "Virtual Private Network" or "VPN" for short.

1) The end user (or employee) has their fingerprint, face, and iris scanned to create the respective verification template. This template then gets broken down into a separate data packet. This data packet (which contains the newly created verification template) is then further encapsulated (or encrypted) into another data packet, so it eventually becomes invisible as it traverses across the various network media, as it makes its way to the servers of the hosting provider;

2) To ensure the integrity of this double-layered data packet, it would also consist of headers which contain information about the size and type of the newly created verification template. This would be a confirmation to the shared resources server that this has not been changed en route;

3) To create another layer of protection, a dedicated VPN channel can be created. This would be a direct line from the point of origin of the fingerprint or iris scanner all the way to the servers of the hosting party. This is known as specifically as "IP Tunneling", and as a result, this channel cannot be seen by other people accessing the Internet across the same network media the data packets (which contains the verification templates) are also traveling across;

4) Once this data packet arrives at the shared resources server, it is then decrypted, and the end user (or employee) can then gain access to the resources they need.

THE HASHING MECHANISM

As it was mentioned in the last section, one of the primary goals of the ZTF (or at least the way that we are proposing it in this book) is to eliminate the need for the end user (or employee) to have been authenticated over and over again. The goal is that they get authenticated once, and that's it. So because of this, the newly created Verification Biometric Template (which can also be referred to as the "Cipher Biometric Template") gets two layers of protection, the first of it being scrambled, and the second, having it encapsulated in second data packet.

But, if the same Verification Template is to be used over and over again, the shared resources need to have confirmation that this template has not been altered or tampered in a way in the transition process. In other words, it has retained its level of integrity, and will need to do so over and over again, until a newer Verification Template has been created.

This is where the Hashing Function comes into use. In simplest terms, it is a mathematical value that is computed at the point of authentication, and is assigned to the data packet that encapsulates the newly created Verification Template. If this value remains the same as it reaches the shared resources server, then one can be assured that the integrity has remained the same. But, if the mathematical value is different for any reason, then that will lead to suspicion that the Verification Template has been altered.

To fix this major security vulnerability, the newly created Verification Template is combined with a "secret key" at the point of authentication first, and then the hash value is created. As a result, this hash will then contain specific information and data about the secret itself. As a result, the shared resourced server can even be further ensured that the Verification Template they have received is the 100% original sent by the authentication server.

This is so because even if the Verification Template, the hash, and the associated secret key were to be intercepted, there is very little that a hacker can do to alter the Verification Template and its associated hash, because they have to have the information and data about the secret key, which is of course something they will never gain access to.

Although the Hashing Mechanism provides for a far greater level of assurance with regards to the integrity of the Verification Template, it is not totally infallible either. Therefore, the use of Quantum Mechanics and Photon Particles, at least in theory, could provide as much as 110% integrity assurances. This will be covered more in Chapter 5 of this book.

The Hashing Function is illustrated below:

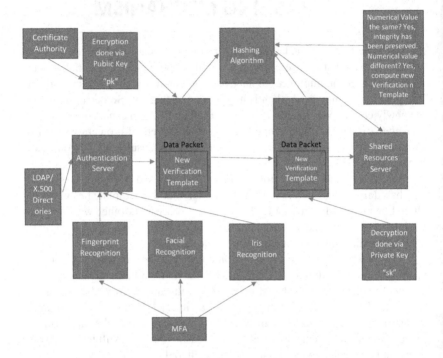

This illustration is reviewed as follows:

1) The end user (or employee is enrolled and verified by MFA, which includes Fingerprint Recognition, Facial Recognition, Iris Recognition).
2) The enrollment template is stored in the database of the Authentication Server (via the LDAP and/or X.500 Directories), and at this point, the end user (or employee) goes through the verification cycle. From here, the first Verification Template is then created. The person in question is fully authenticated.
3) The new Verification Template is a culmination of all three templates after the first verification. It is encapsulated into another data packet, and is encrypted via the Public Key.
4) At the point of authentication, the hashing algorithm and its numerical value are computed.
5) The data packet then makes its way to the shared resources server.

6) It is then decrypted with the Private Key, and access is granted to the end user (or employee) to get to the shared resources that they need to access.

7) Finally, if the numerical value of the Hashing Algorithm remains the same, the Verification Template has remained intact. If not, it has been altered, then the entire process has to be repeated again.

Quantum Physics 4

The first three chapters of this book have reviewed the following topics, which are all very important facets for the development of a Zero Trust Framework:

- The basics of Cryptography;
- Two-Factor Authentication;
- Multifactor Authentication;
- An examination of the key Biometric modalities that can be used for an MFA approach:
  - Fingerprint Recognition
  - Iris Recognition
  - Facial Recognition.

From this point, the book is then distributed into the fact that a Zero Trust Framework does not have a single user approach, as our previous examples in these chapters demonstrated. Rather, in today's environment, especially in the larger businesses, there will be many end users attempting to gain authentication to many other shared resources, across different servers. Thus, the need to have Zero Trust Framework that can handle this load is a must.

Thus, the concept of Asymmetric Key Cryptography was introduced, which is also known as a Public Key Infrastructure or PKI for short. With this newer approach, many end users can be authenticated and authorized to gain access to many shared resources. In of by itself, this kind infrastructure can be resource intense, but in order to streamline this process, other concepts were also introduced:

- Public Keys;
- Private Keys;
- Certificate Authorities;
- LDAP/X.500 Directory structures.

It is the Public Key which encrypts the Biometric Template, and the Private Key which decrypts it. The Certificate Authority serves as the central point in

DOI: 10.1201/9781003392965-4

which the Digital Certificates (also known as the Public Key and Private Key) are issued. Further, they can be used again with some alterations made to them at a subsequent point in time, and thus, these Digital Certificates are stored in the LDAP/X.500 Directories, which serve as the database.

From here, Chapter 4 then delved into the topic of BioCryptography. This is a new and upcoming area of Cybersecurity, and the basic premise of this concept is to further fortify the strength of the Biometric Templates by encrypting them and further encapsulating into another data packet. Further, another goal of the Zero Trust Framework is to create what is known as a passwordless organization.

For example, in the context of the Zero Trust Framework model that we have proposed in this book so far, the same Biometric Template can be used over and over again without having the end user (or the employee) go through the same authentication and authorization processes repeatedly. For example, in the context that we have proposed, an end user (or an employee) would first have to be authenticated by having themselves enrolled first via the three afore-mentioned Biometric modalities.

These newly created Enrollment Templates can be housed in the LDAP/X.500 Directories, but in order to gain access to the shared resources, the end user (employee) would have to go through another cycle, which will then lead to the creation of the Verification Templates. In the end, it is the Enrollment and the Verification Templates which are compared among one another, and if there is a close enough match, then the identity of the end user (employee) is confirmed, and thus, they will be given access to the shared resources server to get access to whatever they are requesting.

But now, imagine having to go through this process each and every time that your employee needs access to the shared resources. Not only would it be a very time-consuming process, but the drain of resources and the processing power of our proposed Zero Trust Framework would also be immense. Therefore, the goal would be to create the ability to keep using the same templates over and over again. Thus, the concepts of Privileged Access Management (PAM) become critical here.

But, as it was reviewed in the last chapter, these different templates that were created will have to be created into one master template, which would then be sent over to the shared resources server for authorization. Because of this, the integrity of this newly created template is absolutely critical. Thus, the concept of Hashing Algorithms was introduced. But these too are prone to a Cyberattack, and because of that, Quantum Mechanics was introduced as a replacement for it. Finally, Chapter 3 concluded with a diagram of what has been reviewed and proposed up to that point in time for our Zero Trust Framework.

We will go back to this very diagram, and from there, add the other key features to our proposed Zero Trust Framework, which are as follows:

1) Privileged Access Management (PAM);
2) Quantum Mechanics (especially that of Quantum Cryptography);
3) Photon Particles.

But first, since this chapter is about the Zero Trust Framework exclusively, it is important to review its origins and its other major facets, other than the ones we have reviewed so far in this book.

THE ORIGINS OF THE ZERO TRUST FRAMEWORK

In reality, the concept of the Zero Trust Framework is nothing new. In fact, it dates back more than a decade ago, all the way to 2010. An individual by the name of John Kindervag developed the philosophy that nothing should be trusted at all, from both within the external and internal environments of a company, or for that matter, any type of entity. The motto here was to get rid all of levels of trust, even how slight it may be. The driving philosophy was to "never trust, but always verify, no matter how many times it has to be done".

Although the concept of the Internet of Things (IoT) was not even heard back during those times, people trying to access connected devices could not be trusted, everybody has to go through the same regimen of verification. John Kindervag even related this concept to Joseph Stalin with his famous quote, "I trust no one, not even myself". Eventually, he named his theory the Zero Trust Framework. Thus, as it will be elaborated more later in this chapter, the Zero Trust Framework is not a "one size fits all" approach.

This means that whatever works for one entity regarding the ZTF will not work for a different one. Rather, it is a methodology that has to be crafted and molded to the exact and unique security requirements of the company.

Probably the first true commercial application of the Zero Trust Framework came back when the United States Office of Personnel Management was hit by a Cyberattack. The House of Representatives mandated the use of the ZTF methodology in order to safeguard not only their digital assets, but also for the rest of the US Federal Government.

Other notable events in the history of the Zero Trust Framework, which have led to its higher levels of adoption today, are stated below.

In 2011

Google came out with its own version of the Zero Trust Framework, and this was called the "BeyondCorp". The main trigger for this was the Cyberattack known as "Operation Aurora", which was launched in 2009. This was deemed to be an Advanced Persistent Threat (also known as "APT"). The premise behind this model was to do away with network segmentation all together, and instead rely upon the use of Multifactor Authentication (MFA) as the main source for both authentication and authorization. More information about Beyond Corp can be seen at the link below:

https://www.beyondcorp.com/

In 2014, Google published a whitepaper about their proposed framework, which gave a rather big boost to the overall concepts of the Zero Trust Framework. This is deemed to be an important piece of work, and it can be downloaded and viewed at this link:

http://cyberresources.solutions/ZTF_Book/Beyond_Corp.pdf

In 2018

Forrester came up with their own model of the Zero Trust Framework, which was entitled the "Zero Trust eXtended Ecosystem". This methodology consisted of seven different layers, which are as follows:

- Workforce Security;
- Device Security;
- Workload;
- Network;
- Data Security;
- Visibility and Analytics;
- Automation and Orchestration.

Also, the National Institute of Standards and Technology came out with yet their own version of the Zero Trust Framework and this was released as Special Publication 800-207. Subsequently in 2020, this publication was updated.

In 2019

Gartner, in a manner similar to that of Forrester, also launched their version of the Zero Trust Framework, which was called the "Zero Trust Network Access" (also known as the "ZTNA"). In return, this also gave birth to a new Cyber concept (and even tool) called the "Secure Access Service Edge", also more commonly known as "SASE". The premise of this is that any processing and transactions of datasets occur close to the device that is requesting these services, rather than having them done at the central database server.

In 2021

Another major catalyst for the adoption of the Zero Trust Framework was the COVID-19 pandemic. With everybody now working from home, businesses were seeking new ways in which to counter the new threat variants which persisted. In fact, according to a research report which was published by Microsoft entitled the "Zero Trust Adoption Report", an overwhelming 96% of the 1200 respondents polled said that they favored the concepts of the overall concepts of the Zero Trust Framework.

From 2021 to Present

The Biden Administration has been the main trigger during this time frame, with the following events being the main drivers:

- Executive Order on Improving the Nation's Cybersecurity: This was signed in May 2021, with the main intention of enhancing the security posture of the US Federal Government and the nation's Critical Infrastructure.
- The U.S. Office of Management and Budget (also known as the "OMB") further endorsed the adoption of the Zero Trust Framework.
- The Cybersecurity and Infrastructure Security Agency (also known as the "CISA") also came out with a different version of the Zero Trust Framework, and it was called the "Cloud Security Technical Reference Architecture and Zero Trust Maturity Model". This methodology focused more upon Cloud-based security, especially focusing on data leakages, whether intentional or not.
- The Acting Director of the OMB (Shalanda D. Young) gave Federal Agencies until the end of the Fiscal Year of 2024 to deploy and implement certain controls to fulfill the following objectives of their own version of the Zero Trust Framework:
  - Identity;
  - Devices;
  - Networks;
  - Applications and Data.
- The CISA came and published the second version of their Cloud Security/Zero Trust Framework Publication. It can be downloaded and viewed here:
  http://cyberresources.solutions/ZTF_Book/CISA_Publication.pdf
- Okta conducted a major market research project which was entitled "The State of Zero Trust Security 2022." It was discovered that at least

72% of all of the Federal Agencies had some sort of Zero Trust plan in place, or they were at least working on the first drafts of one.

*(SOURCE: https://www.techtarget.com/whatis/feature/
History-and-evolution-of-zero-trust-security)*

The origins of the Zero Trust Framework can be summarized in the illustration below:

For the longest time, businesses have adopted what is known as "Perimeter Security". A technical definition for it is as follows:

> Perimeter security is the philosophy of setting up functional apparatus or techniques at the perimeter of the network to secure data and resources.
>
> *(SOURCE: https://www.techopedia.com/definition/33764/ perimeter-security)*

In other words, imagine one large circle encompassing a business, which is the main line of defense. That can be thought of as Perimeter Security. It is from within the confines of this circle that a business will deploy all of the firewalls, network intrusion devices, routers, etc., as well as other types of security technologies in order to fortify their defenses. It is also at this point that the authentication mechanisms will be deployed, especially from the standpoint of Physical Access Entry. This is illustrated in the diagram below:

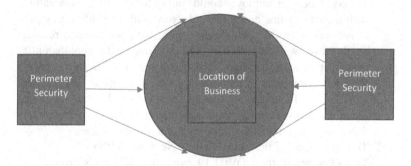

With this kind of approach to security, there was always an implicit level of trust that was recognized. For example, if you were an employee gaining access to shared resources, it was always assumed that you went through all of the authentication processes that were in place. Even if you were a third-party vendor, the vetting process was very easy and simple to get through, because there was an implicit layer of trust that no intentional harm would ever be done to the datasets or the business processes that were being outsourced. In other words, the main concern was protecting the organization from threats that were coming from the external environment.

Nobody was really ever concerned about the internal environment of the business, because after all, once again, if you were an employee, nobody really paid too much attention to your specific rights, permissions, and privileges. It was always assumed that you were given the right amount to do your daily job tasks. Because of this, the thoughts of an Insider Attack from precipitating were pretty much null.

But, there is one major problem with the Perimeter Security approach. This model assumes only layer of security. Thus, if the Cyberattacker were to penetrate through it, you then have pretty much given away the keys to the crown jewels of your company, because there are no other layers of security located from within the confines of the business.

There are other reasons for the eventual erosion of the Perimeter Security model, which are as follows:

1) The remote workforce

   Many people thought that a 100% Remote Workforce would transpire later this decade. But instead, the COVID-19 pandemic made this into a reality within just a 3-month timespan. With the influx of workers now working from home, there were many security issues that transpire. One of the largest ones was the intermingling of both the corporate network with the home-based networks. Gone were the days where an employee could simply log into their workstation with their username and password. Now, with two different types of network infrastructures touching base with one another, remote employees now absolutely had to be confirmed with more than just one layer of authentication. As a result, many IT Security teams were left scrambling to implement a system where at least two or more layers of authentication would be required. This proved to be a major catalyst for the companies to start at least thinking about deploying the Zero Trust Framework in a serious manner.

2) The breakdown of the Virtual Private Network (VPN)

   The VPN before the COVID-19 pandemic hit always provided a secure way for employees to remotely login into the servers where the shared resources were held. But during these times, only about 25-30% of employees were actually working remotely. But with the rapid influx to a near 99% Remote Workforce, the VPN started to show its breaking points. As a result, the Cyberattacker was able to exploit new weaknesses in a legacy system. Once again, using two or more layers of authentication and the concept of "Never Trust, Always Verify" took even further hold.

3) The race to the Cloud

   Along with the issue of the intermingling of corporate and home-based networks, many remote employees were given company-issued devices that were not properly fitted with adequate security protocols installed onto them. Because of this, and other reasons, many businesses started to migrate their On Premises Infrastructures into the major Cloud-based platforms, such as that of the AWS and Microsoft Azure. Since this was an unknown territory for many organizations, especially for the SMBs, many of them chose to utilize the Private Cloud deployment because of the security that was afforded. But as familiarity with the Cloud started to settle in, many of them subsequently started to move out to the Hybrid Cloud model. This is essentially a combination of the Private Cloud and Public Cloud. But since lines access and separation were not too clear, many login credentials became at risk here, as the IT Security teams struggled to keep track which end user (or employee) accounts needed to be created, and those which had to be deleted and/or deprovisioned. Even to this day, this is a big problem, as data leakage issues have emerged, especially with the AWS S3 buckets. This is an area now in which the IT Security teams are starting to realize, which needs much more attention, especially through the use of automation. The use of PAM in a Zero Trust Framework is a solution, and as mentioned earlier, it will be explored in more detail later in this chapter.

4) Artificial Intelligence (AI) and Machine Learning (ML)

The last couple of years have a seen a huge rise in both of these technologies, especially when it comes to automation. This concept just does not apply to manufacturing scenarios (this is where Robotic Process Automation comes into play), but it can also apply to virtual processes as well, such as when it comes to optimizing and parsing through large datasets (which is also known as "Big Data"). For example, if there is one Virtual Machine (VM), which has SQL Server running and another VM that is running an Oracle Enterprise database, and they both are conducting automated tasks, there cannot be any kind of accidental data interchange between the two servers. Thus, only a Zero Trust Framework can help prevent this from happening, as these VMs can be segregated from one another by their own boundaries.

THE DEMISE OF PERIMETER SECURITY

In the end, the ultimate goal of Perimeter Security was to keep all assets, whether they were digital, physical, or intellectual within the confines of the business, and the Perimeter Defense would contain them there, and provide protection under just one layer of security. But given the reasons in the last subsection, as well as other factors (such as the rise of Insider Attacks and the overwhelming amount of threat variants from the external environment constantly pounding it), the demise of Perimeter Security finally happened.

Now, with offices and employees around the world and working in a virtual-based environment, the Perimeter Security Model will now no longer suffice. This scattering of assets and resources for a company can be seen below:

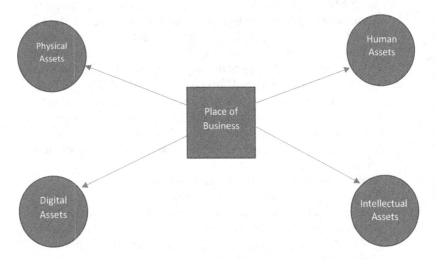

As a result, since everything is scattered all over the world, any kind of trust cannot be afforded anymore, thus fueling the demand for the Zero Trust Framework even more.

THE EMERGENCE OF THE ZERO TRUST FRAMEWORK

So far in this chapter, we have provided a history of the evolution of the Zero Trust Framework and reviewed the factors that led to the eventual demise (or almost near collapse) of the Perimeter Security Model. Thus going forward, we now assume that the Zero Trust Framework will be the methodology of choice for not only keeping the IT and Network infrastructure secure for an organization, but is also one of the most optimal ways in the authentication and authorization for end users (or employees) to gain access to shared resources, and other types of confidential assets.

Before we resume with the initial Zero Trust Framework model we introduced at the end of Chapter 4, it is important to know some of the key properties of what truly makes up this framework. Some of these properties are as follows:

1) It depends on risk

   Theoretically speaking, you want to protect everything that is of at risk in your business. But in a real-world sense, we know that this totally infeasible. You can only give the highest levels of protection to those assets that are the most vulnerable to a security breach. Now, the question arises as to how to decide what is weak? One of the best ways to figure this out is for you and your IT Security team to take an inventory of all of the assets that your company has (both digital and physical), and breaking them down into the different categories that they belong to. Once this has been completed, you can then rank them on a scale, perhaps where 1 = Least Vulnerable and 10 = Most Vulnerable. Anything in the intermediate range would get a medium ranking. Now, you take all of those assets and from there determine the appropriate controls that they need. The bottom line here is that the depth of your Zero Trust Framework will be dependent upon how many vulnerable assets you have, and how much they worth that they have for the organization. Meaning if you have a lot of them, you will need to break out your IT and Network Infrastructure into more, smaller units. But if you are a smaller business, you may not have as many assets on hand, thus the need for segmentation will not be as high, and you will need a lesser number of units that are to be divided.

2) Repeated use of MFA

   A constant theme throughout this book, especially in Chapters 3 and 4, has been the repeated use of MFA. For each and everything you need to access to, you must keep getting reauthenticated and reauthorized. This is also a core element of the Zero Trust Framework. While once again in theory this is probably the best way to fortify your lines of defense, following this procedure in the real world could prove to be very ineffective. For example, in the Public Key Infrastructure (PKI) methodology that we have proposed, there will be an enormous drain on both resources and processing power. Therefore, one of the goals is to introduce Privileged Access Management (also known as "PAM") which will allow for the end user (or employee) to have to through the entire authentication and authorization only once. This will also be reviewed in greater detail later in this chapter.

3) Endpoints are further protected

One of the major pitfalls of the Perimeter Security Model is that the Endpoint Security has often been a forgotten about topic. Essentially, the endpoints are the points of origination and termination for the network lines of communication. Since they have been ignored for such a long period of time, this has been a favorite point of entry for the Cyberattacker to penetrate into an IT and Network Infrastructure. As a result, they have been able to stay in for long periods of time, and move laterally in a covert fashion. Because of this, they also have been to exfiltrate data a bit at a time, very often going unnoticed, until it was too late. But, of the strategic advantages of the Zero Trust Framework is that this is no longer an issue. In other words, Endpoint Security is a very crucial component that cannot be forgotten about.

4) Isolation

With the Perimeter Defense model, not only was it much easier for a Cyberattacker to get in, but it was also easier for them to get out of the system if they have been detected. But this is not the case with the Zero Trust Framework. Because the IT and Network Infrastructure is broken up into different segments, it makes that much more difficult for the Cyberattacker to get through the crown jewels of the organization. But by the time he or she has broken through any lines of defense, the IT Security team will have alerted, and corrective action would have followed immediately. Thus, there are very good chances that the Cyberattacker will be isolated with no point of exit possible.

5) Finer levels of control

Under Perimeter Defense, for the most part, the concept of Least Privilege was followed. But most of the rights, permissions, and privileges were of a "macro" one, meaning that it was quite possible for an end user (or employee) to still access other applications when they had no reason to. In other words, people were put into various groups and profiles into an Active Directory structure with the rights, permissions, and privileges already preestablished into it. There were no finer controls established to prevent unintended access to other systems. This becomes especially crucial for those Privileged Accounts. Thus, another key mandate of the Zero Trust Framework is to establish a granular (or finer) set of controls that will eliminate this kind of crossover to other applications.

6) Comprehensive auditing

Most companies set up their Perimeter Security to only audit certain parts of their IT Network Infrastructures. Most of them were set up to only monitor the flow of network traffic in and out of the business, and to detect any rouge data packets. It wasn't until recently when the interest of detecting malicious or unusual behavior picked up, with the advent of both AI and ML tools. But with the Zero Trust Framework, and especially for those deployed in a Cloud-based environment, there are now tools available that give the IT Security team the ability to audit everything in their respective infrastructures. This also includes the ever important endpoints, and even the ability to track a wireless device on a real-time basis, and even obtain a log file from that. Also with Perimeter Defense, the IT Security team traditionally had to comb through all of the log files that were outputted on a manual basis. Compounding this fact was that security tools came from different vendors, and as a result of that, different formats were created. But now, and with the growth of the Zero Trust Framework, a central console can be used (which is a Security Incident Event Manager, or "SIEM" for short) to see the outputs of all of the log files from one central location.

7) The use of adaptive control

The common way to detect any sort of malicious or rogue behavior under the Perimeter Security Model was to create a simple baseline and from there, upon the thresholds set by the IT Security team, anything outside of what was deemed to be normal would require further attention. But this would often trigger what are known as "false positives". In order to alleviate this situation, there are other variables that have to be taken into account in order to determine true, rogue behavior. These are as follows:

- Time of the day;
- Day of the week;
- Geographic location;
- IP Address;
- Target Server;
- Target Application.

These kinds of specifications are more or less required by a Zero Trust Framework, and to be conducted on a real-time basis. The variables just examined above are also technically known as "Adaptive Controls".

8) Contextual request

With implicit trust being used in a Perimeter Defense Model, any elevation of privileges, rights, and permissions was often granted without a second thought, especially for the privileged accounts. But since the Zero Trust Framework means absolutely no trust whatsoever, the granting of super user permissions can only take place if only questions such as the entity who is requesting this, the target server, why this kind of access is needed, and for how long it will be required have all been answered.

9) Lateral movement

Since there are many layers of security in the Zero Trust Framework, the lateral movement of a Cyberattacker is almost nil after even penetrating the first one or two layers. This is unlike the Perimeter Defense Model, while after piercing through the first and only line of defense, the Cyberattacker will have complete reign in the IT and Network Infrastructure.

The Basic Zero Trust Framework Model

Now that we have reviewed some of the most properties of the Zero Trust Framework, it is now at this point we into actually present the basic model of the Zero Trust Framework. Once again, keep that this is a methodology, and it is not meant to be a cookie cutter approach to security. Businesses can modify to it, by making additions to it as they see necessary.

The Model

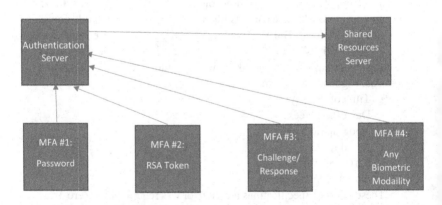

This can be deemed to be the most fundamental model of the Zero Trust Framework. For example, it first embraces MFA, in which at least three more mechanisms are used. In the scenario above, there are four of them, and there are three types of identification criterion that are met in this case, which are as follows:

1) Something you are

This is typically something that is permanent about you, such as your physiological or behavioral self. This is where Biometrics (reviewed in Chapter 3) will come into play (which is MFA #4).

2) Something you know
   This is a piece of information and/or data that you know of. It can be a password, an answer to a challenge/response question, etc. These are represented as MFA #1, and MFA #3, respectively.
3) Something you have
   This is something in your position such as an RSA Token, smart card, FOB, etc. This is represented as MFA #2.

Once the end user (or employee) has gone through all of these iterations, he or she will then be granted access to whatever shared resources they need to conduct their daily job tasks. But the caveat here is that each time the end user wants to gain access to something else or different, they have to go through this entire process once again. And, if this happens multiple times in a single day (which is highly probable), then it will not only be a cumbersome process, but it can also be a drain of processing power on part of the Authentication Server.

In our proposed model of the Zero Trust Framework, we theoretically do away with this repetitive cycle by making use of the concepts of PAM. As mentioned, this will be reviewed in more detail later in this chapter.

Because of the almost near eradication of the Perimeter Defense Model, this has left many businesses in what is called as an "amorphous state". Meaning, there are no clear-cut boundaries as to where all of the digital assets now lie at; they are now technically speaking in different physical locations, but virtually, they look like they are all in one place, if you are using a Cloud-based deployment. This now gives rise to a very important concept for the traditional Zero Trust Framework Model: Segmentation.

What Is Segmentation?

When one thinks of this concept, the image of a large unit being broken into smaller bits often comes to mind. This is true of the Zero Trust Framework. A technical definition of Segmentation is as follows:

> It is a network security technique that divides a network into smaller, distinct sub-networks that enable network teams to compartmentalize the sub-networks and deliver unique security controls and services to each sub-network.
>
> The process of network segmentation involves partitioning a physical network into different logical sub-networks. Once the network has been subdivided into smaller more manageable units, controls are applied to the individual, compartmentalized segments.
>
> *(SOURCE: https://www.vmware.com/topics/glossary/content/ network-segmentation.html)*

Although the entire processes and operation of a business can be broken into smaller units or segments, it is typically the IT and Network Infrastructure that is broken down, because it is deemed to be the most vital component (or "heart and soul") of any enterprise. So now, imagine all of those digital assets (this can be everything from the data bases to the Virtual Machines to the Virtual Desktops to all of the datasets, etc.) that are now in existence in any kind of Cloud deployment (again, they are the Private, Public, and Hybrid Clouds).

Per the permutations and requirements that have been set forth by the IT Security team and the CISO, all of them now will reside into smaller units, or what will now be termed as "Segments". Each of these segments will be surrounded by their own boundary, with all of the authentication mechanisms which support the MFA protocols. In more technical terms, these can also be referred to as "Subnets", as eluded to in the previous definition. These Segments can still be, on a theoretical level, broken down into smaller ones, which become known as "Microsegments".

It is important to note at this point that this model of the Zero Trust Framework (and even those going forward) requires that the authentication methods that are being used *be different from one another.* This means that for each boundary that encompasses a certain Segment, all the MFA mechanisms used must be totally different from one another. For example, one could still be a password, one could be a smart card, and the other could be a Biometric.

But the only caveat here is that there are a finite number of authentication mechanisms that can go around. But even with this, there are still quite a number of possibilities in which you can set up your MFA strategies. For example, you could take the MFA from one layer and use them three layers up or down in the segmented IT/Network Infrastructure. Also, the Zero Trust Framework mandates that the same authentication methods for supporting the MFA should not be used for long periods of time. They once again should follow a regular schedule of randomization by swapping them out to a pre-established plan.

Probably the most important keywords to remember with the Zero Trust Framework are that of Trajectory and Isolation. With the former, even though the Cyberattacker might be able to break through one or two, and perhaps even three layers of defense, the chances of he or she getting to the proverbial crown jewels become almost statistically nil. With the latter, once a Cyberattacker has broken though, the chances of him or her breaking out again are also almost nil because they will be facing the issue of Isolation because of the other layers of defense that will be surrounding them.

The illustration below gives a three-dimensional picture of what Segmentation looks like, especially in the highlighted areas:

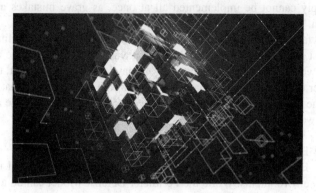

But, this basic model of the Zero Trust Framework does not include the following components of our proposed model, which include the following:

1) The Public Key Infrastructure;
2) Privileged Access Management;
3) BioCryptography;
4) Quantum Mechanics.

As mentioned previously, these above four components will be examined in more detail toward the end of this chapter. But while we are still on this theme of the basic Zero Trust Framework model, the next sections of this chapter will cover the following topics:

- The advantages/disadvantages of the Zero Trust Framework;
- Best practices in deploying a basic Zero Trust Framework Model at your business.

THE ADVANTAGES OF THE
ZERO TRUST FRAMEWORK

Although the basic model of the Zero Trust Framework may sound very complex in nature because of all of the Segmenting that will be going on, and all of the MFA authentication mechanisms that will be deployed, once it is established, it won't appear to be that way. But the key here is that whatever Zero Trust Framework Model you deploy, it will have to be deployed in phases. It simply cannot be implemented all at once, as grave mistakes are sure to happen.

In fact, there will be a section later in this chapter that will outline some of the best practices that you can take to deploy the basic model of the Zero Trust Framework. But despite how complex it may look from the outset, there are a number of key advantages that will far outweigh even the ones that are found with the Perimeter Defense Model. Here are some of benefits of the Zero Trust Framework:

1) Both kinds of threats are mitigated

By this, we mean the threats from both the external and internal environments. While the Perimeter Defense Model can do a suffice job with the former for a period of time, it does not offer a means by which threats from the internal environment can be tracked. By this, we mean the Insider Attacks. This kind of threat vector can stem from any kind of source, but the common denominator here is that it usually takes an employee from the inside to launch this kind of attack. After all, he or she knows best the internal workings of a company (this depends on their specific job role), and they will of course have some idea as to where the damage can be initiated. For example, this can be an employee who feels that they are about to lose their job, or through a Social Engineering tactic, there could be somebody from the outside world conning an employee to launch such a threat vector. Under the traditional security practices, it is very difficult to detect the beginning of an Insider Attack. At best, the log files will alert the IT Security team for unusual behavior, but this is really not enough to tell with accuracy if anything is about to happen. But with the Zero Trust Framework, the key here is not to only protect from threat vectors that are posed from the external environments, *but those that are internal as well*. Given all the internal boundaries, and the many authentication mechanisms, it will be a lot easier now to detect the precipitation of an Insider Attack. In other words, with the Zero Trust Framework, the business is protected from different kinds of environments, which is a huge advantage to have.

2) Can see all of the actions

Before the COVID-19 pandemic hit, a lot of the IT Security teams did not pay too much attention to the kinds of types of devices that the employees were using, although they should have been. But once it happened, the fears then quickly arose who was accessing what through which device, driven primarily because of the intermeshing of both the business and home networks. Another trigger point for this Bring Your Own Device (BYOD), where remote employees were very often using their own personal device to conduct their daily job tasks, rather than making use of the company issued equipment. With the Zero Trust Framework, a much closer eye can be kept on the devices that are being used to access the shared resources. This is so because each device must now be registered with the IT Security team, and since now MFA will be used, it will be much more difficult for employees to access anything through their personal devices. Also, since all network-based activities can be seen through a central console, the IT Security team will now be able to track down lost or stolen devices and from that point issue a "Remote Wipe" command to permanently delete any confidential information or data that may have been stored on it. Remember that in the end,

3) Reduction in data loss

This has always been an issue, even before the COVID-19 pandemic hit. But once it was completely unleashed, the issue of data leakage, whether intentional or not, became a much graver concern. For example, most of the home networks that were being used to access the business network were only using a password as the primary means of defense. This constituted for a weak defense, at best. As a result, the Cyberattacker could very easily have broken through this line of access, and moved laterally into the business network. From here, depending upon where they were at, they could then stay in long enough to see where the datasets reside at, and which ones were the most valuable to exfiltrate. Of course, they are not going to do all of this at once; they are going to take out these datasets a bit at a time, to go unnoticed. But if the Zero Trust Framework had been implemented during this time frame, the fear of data loss would have been greatly diminished, because of all of the layers of defenses that the Cyberattacker would have to literally go through. Plus, each defense layer will also have its own set of controls, thus making data loss/exfiltration an almost impossible task to accomplish.

4) Security is better at the Cloud

As it has been mentioned throughout this book, many organizations have been moving to the Cloud and migrating their On Prem infrastructure totally into it. Not only does it afford monthly pricing, but one of the key strategies is that it is highly scalable. For example, if you do have a Zero Trust Framework that is in the Cloud, it is quite easy to break out new assets into their own distinctive segments, as well as deploying the appropriate MFA protocols and authentication mechanisms into place. If for some reason any assets have to be deleted or deprovisioned, the Zero Trust Framework will adjust accordingly, on an automatic basis without any human intervention involved. Also, the major Cloud Providers, especially that of Microsoft Azure, already have a suite of MFA tools that can be installed and deployed with just a few clicks of the mouse. However, it should be noted that the debate between having a Zero Trust Framework in the Cloud versus it being On Premises will always be a continuing one. But making changes to it with the latter will obviously take longer, which is something no organization can afford. Thus, the choice is quite clear in this regard.

5) A newer type of workforce model

The workforce when the COVID-19 pandemic hit was almost all remote based. This meant that people could work from anywhere, in their homes, or even in any other public location, as long as there was a secure Internet connection. But, as the pandemic started to ease down, many businesses started to reopen their doors. However, a majority of the remote employees preferred to work from the physical location of their office only a few days a week. Thus, this gave birth to a newer type of workforce model, called the "Hybrid Model", where the remote worker would spend one or two days in the office, and the rest of the time would be spent working from home. Because of this, many of these businesses then transferred their Cloud deployment to Hybrid one as well. With this kind of approach, if a Perimeter Defense Model were to be used, it would be much more difficult to keep track of where all of the devices were being used at, and which end user (or employee) was accessing which shared resources. But by using the Cloud, the Zero Trust Framework can easily keep track of these geographically separated devices, and ensure that MFA is still being used on them. But, the only issue here is keeping track of all of the accounts and profiles in the Azure Activity Directory. But this where the role of PAM will come into play.

6) Supports compliance across the board

The world today is filled with various data privacy laws. Some of the most well-known ones are those of the GDPR, the CCPA, and HIPAA. Depending upon their revenue and employee size, companies will have to come under the tight scrutinization of regulators from each of these laws. If the right controls are not in place, or there are any data leakage issues, the company will be in the cross hairs for an audit and possible steep financial penalties. But with the Zero Trust Framework, since there are so many controls and authentication mechanisms put into place (especially if you are using a Cloud-based deployment), there is a much greater chance that you will more or less be in compliance with these various data privacy laws, and experience a much lower risk of data exfiltration issues.

THE DISADVANTAGES OF THE ZERO TRUST FRAMEWORK

Despite the strategic advantages that the Zero Trust Framework brings to an organization, it also has its set of disadvantages. Some of these include the following:

1) It is viewed as extreme

   To an end user (or an employee), the Zero Trust Framework is often perceived as going way too far to the other extreme in security. But unfortunately, despite all of the best efforts to provide employees with security awareness training and trying to keep up with the Cyber Threat landscape, there is really no other choice. There is a lot at stake here for the CISO, as well as other members of the C-Suite and even the Board of Directors, which are namely the protection of the digital assets and the confidential datasets of both the employees and customers. The situation of Zero Trust has been for a lack of a better term, forced upon us, given the dynamics that we are facing today. We simply cannot take anything for granted anymore, because the Cyberattacker has also become a lot stealthier and covert in the way they launch their threat vectors. Some of the people that will feel the worst brunt of the Zero Trust Framework will be those that have been around the longest in a company. Given their long tenure, there is obviously a lot of trust that has been placed with them. But to have that taken all that taken away at once and then not trust them at all (from the standpoint of authentication and authorization) can be traumatic. Therefore, one of the key aspects when deploying a Zero Trust Framework is to keep a direct line of communications open with the end users (or employees) and all levels of management, and vice versa. It is very important to get their buy in even to the slightest degree possible, and explain the benefits of what it is all about. If this is not done properly, resentment toward the Zero Trust Framework will get even worse, and your end users (or employees) may try to circumvent the system all together, thus defeating its very purpose. One way to alleviate this situation is to deploy your Zero Trust Framework in phases, as it was pointed out to earlier in this chapter. By taking this kind of approach, you will be giving your end users (or employees) a time period to digest the new changes that will be happening to them. Although it may take a lot longer to completely build out your Zero Trust Framework to its entirety, the slower the pace the better, at least from the standpoint of end user (or employee) adoption.

2) The use of Micro Segmentation

As it was explained in great detail, the use of the Zero Trust Framework relies heavily upon the concept of Segmentation. Once again, this is where the entire IT and Network Infrastructure is divided up into separate segments, with each of them being surrounded by its own boundary, and MFA authentication tools. But if the organization is a very large one, and if the Zero Trust Framework has proven to be successful, the CISO and the IT Security team could consider making use of what is known as "Microsegmentation". This is where the given Segment is broken down yet into an even smaller one. A benefit in this of course is an extra added layer of security. But if it is deployed for no other reason, it can cause more complication to an already existing Zero Trust Framework. Therefore, any other major tweaks or adjustments like this should only be done if there is some success that has been proven with it initially. In other words, don't add any more to your Zero Trust Framework until it has given you a positive ROI for the time and money you have spent into it initially.

3) A mix of environments

Although many organizations have made their full shift to the Cloud, there are some still out there that are hesitant to do this, so they have resorted what is known as a "Mixed Model". This is where they may use part of the Cloud for some of their IT and Network Infrastructure, and the rest still remains On Prem. While this approach may work for some time, it is certainly not a suitable one for the Zero Trust Framework. In other words, it can't be deployed in half in one environment and half in another kind. It has to be implemented fully, and in only one type of environment. One of the reasons for this is that it will be a lot harder to keep track of all of the MFA mechanisms that are in place, as well as of the accesses that are being made to the shared resources. Therefore, before even starting to deploy a Zero Trust Framework, you as the CISO, and your IT Security team need to assess the best kind of environment a Zero Trust Framework will work for you. Then, you need to plan accordingly. But, if there are any lingering thoughts about making a full migration to the Cloud, you should do that first, and then consider the creation of a Zero Trust Framework. But it is also important to keep in mind that a Zero Trust Framework may not even be a viable solution for some businesses, especially those that are classified as a "Small Business" (around 15 employees or less). In these cases, perhaps just using a Two-Factor Authentication (2FA) could work as well too.

4) Some flexibility is required

Although the Zero Trust Framework is inherently designed to be a tight knit kind of environment, there may be some degree of flexibility that is needed in the initial outlay of it, as your end users (or employees) are starting to get used to a brand new way of accessing resources that they need. But you and your IT Security team should not let your guard down, as this could be pivotal moment for the Cyberattacker to penetrate into walls of defenses. But even after this, depending upon the job roles that your remote employees have, there may be a need for some flexibility. This will be especially true for those that are deemed to be the "Road Warriors", and need access to applications and/or resources they need immediately to which they never had before.

5) The IoT

This is an acronym that stands for the "Internet of Things". Essentially, this is where all of the objects that we interact with in both the physical and digital worlds are all interconnected together. While the IoT has a certain number of key advantages for personal applications (such as the "Smarthome", the "Smart Car", etc.), it can pose a serious threat to business applications and processes, and even to the Zero Trust Framework. The primary reason for this is that many of the interconnections in the world of the IoT are often insecure as they remain unencrypted. In other words, any communications that take place between devices, and any authentication/authorization credentials (such as your username/password, PIN number, etc.) are sent as a "Cleartext", which is decipherable to anybody. If this were to be intercepted by a malicious third party, just about anything disastrous can happen. Also, if any of these IoT devices were connected to a Zero Trust Framework without any prior authorization from the IT Security team, this could yet be another avenue for the Cyberattacker to get in, at least through the first layer of defense.

Now that we have reviewed some of the key advantages and disadvantages of the Zero Trust Framework, we now turn our attention over to a set of best practices that should be at least taken into consideration when deploying the basic model of it.

SOME OF THE BEST PRACTICES

Although the Zero Trust Framework model we have been reviewing thus far in this chapter has been the basic one, there are still a number of key points to keep in mind when you deploy it. Also remember that this methodology is not designed to be a "one size fits all". Meaning what will work for one environment will not work for yours. As mentioned, a lot will depend upon the Risk Assessment that you and your IT Security team have compiled at a previous point in time, and the appropriate set of controls you have decided upon as a result.

Here are some of these key tips:

1) Form a Zero Trust Team
   Before you even start to draft out a plan for deploying the Zero Trust Framework at your organization, you first need to create a team with the key stakeholders in mind. Obviously, this will consist of you, the CISO, and a representative member of the IT Security team. Keep in mind that this is a methodology which will have an impact on everybody in the business. Therefore, it would be best to also include a representative from the other departments. Perhaps even consider including a member of the C-Suite, and the IT Department as well. The purpose of this team is to address all of the concerns and needs of the organization, and how you plan start the buy in process from the other employees. Although in theory the Zero Trust Framework in theory can be used by any business, in practicality, it may not be the most suitable approach for a business. Therefore, this is something that should be discussed as well before moving forward. Also, the impacts of a Zero Trust Framework on the technological components and the digital assets that your organization has need to be taken into very serious consideration as well. But, this is a more urgent matter if you still have an On Premises Infrastructure. If you have a Cloud-based deployment, then this topic may not be as important to discuss, as templates and strategies should be available to you from your Cloud Provider in guiding you with this process.

2) Assess the environments that you are in
   By this, if you are 100% in the Cloud, you and your IT Security team need to take a very accurate stock of where digital assets are at in terms of the deployments that you are using. For example, is all of your IT and Network Infrastructure located in just the Private, Hybrid, or Public cloud, or is it segregated amongst all three or just

two of them? Or if you are still using an On Premises Infrastructure, in which areas do you have your servers, workstations, and wireless devices. From here, it is important to create a high-level map as to where everything is located. This will then form as the foundation as to how you will create the various Segments in your IT and Network Infrastructure. Another key advantage of using the Cloud is that you will have tools at your disposal to map this out fairly quickly.

3) Decide the authentication tools

If after completing the first two steps the decision is a "yes" to go with the creation of a Zero Trust Framework, then an important next step is to decide upon the kinds and types of authentication mechanisms that you and your IT Security team think will work best for the security requirements of your company. Some of the favored ones are the use of passwords, challenge/response questions, smart cards, FOBs, RSA tokens, Biometrics, etc. In fact, with some of these tools, there will be other complimentary tools that you can use as well. For example, there are other technologies that are similar with the RSA token, and you can use those in conjunction with RSA one as well. Although we have detailed the Biometric modalities of choice for a Zero Trust Framework in Chapter 3, there are still others that you can choose from, but keep in mind that they are not all commercially available yet. Another important tool that you can give serious consideration and which is widely available is known as the "SASE". This is an acronym that stands for "Secure Access Service Edge". This is a SaaS-based device that creates and deploys a Virtual Machine (VM) near the devices that are requesting access to the shared resources, and processing of data. The idea is by having it closer to the end user (or employee), the transmission and transaction times will be quicker, respectively. A theoretical illustration of the SASE is illustrated below:

4) Develop your Zero Trust Framework Plan

Once you have decided the authentication mechanisms as reviewed, the next step is to actually map as to how your Zero Trust Framework will like, going into the granular detail as much as possible. Think of this as the security blueprint for your company. In this set of documents, you should establish every Segment in your IT and Network Infrastructure, as well as the authentication tools that will be used. There are two key things to keep in mind here:

• This is a set of documents which is still theoretical in nature. So far, they have not been tested in a real-world environment. Therefore, you and your IT Security team need to literally test each and every Segment in a sandbox-like environment to make sure that it is working up to expectations, and that there are no glitches which are involved. If there are any, then it must be remediated immediately. Once one Segment has been deemed to optimal, then it can be released into the production environment where your end users (or employees) will start the MFA approach in order to gain access to the shared resources that they are seeking.

• By taking the above approach, you will actually be developing the plan as to how it will phase in your Zero Trust Framework. True, you and your IT Security team can test all of the Segments in the sandbox all at once, and deploy them into production that same way also, but errors are prone to happen, which could have a detrimental and cascading effect on the other layers of security. Therefore, and as also stated previously in this chapter, the Zero Trust Framework must be implemented in steps, or in phases, to minimize any kind of downtime to your business. So, the bottom line here is to test each component separately, and then deploy it.

5) The complete deployment

At some point in time, after all of the diagramming, documentation, and testing, your Zero Trust Framework should be up and running in its full entirety. But keep in mind that it does not end just there. Rather, you and your IT Security team, as well as the other key stakeholders (as identified in the first step) need to keep a close eye on how things are working. If there are any issues (there will most likely be some in the first few months of actual deployment), they need to be investigated and rectified immediately before they are transmitted to the other segments of the Zero Trust Framework, if at all. Each segment of it will be independent from this, so this risk should be minimal in terms of actual occurrence. But apart from this, your team should also be kept apprised of other new kinds of tools which emerge onto the marketplace that could potentially be used in a Zero Trust Framework. Keep in mind that you want your model to be as updated as possible in terms of newer technologies, as well as having a regular software patch/update schedule for your authentication mechanisms. In fact, if it is feasible for your organization, you may even want to consider having a dedicated Zero Trust Framework team whose primary purpose is to keep tabs with what is going on and make recommendations for improvement.

6) Always seek approval:

As your Zero Trust Framework Model continues to evolve throughout your business, keep in mind that changes and refinements will always be made to keep up with the latest threat vectors that are appearing on the Cyber landscape. But, one simply cannot change something when they want to. Rather there has to be a solid system of checks and balances in place. This is where the Change Configuration Committee comes into place. Every request for a change or an upgrade must be brought up and approved at this level. Any action taken must also be documented, not only for the sake of compliance, but to also abide by the tenets of the various data privacy laws (such as the GDPR, CCPA, HIPAA, etc.).

Keep in mind that there are also key metrics that you can use to gauge the true effectiveness of your Zero Trust Framework Model. Some of these include the following:

1) "Mean time to detect (MTTD):
   This is a crucial element because the faster an organization identifies an attack, the greater the odds it can contain it with minimal damage.
2) Mean time to respond (MTTR):
   The ability to neutralize a threat and get systems back online is critical because as events drag out, risks and costs increase.
3) Mean time to contain (MTTC):

This metric refers to the average time required to shut down all attack vectors across all endpoints and minimize the probability of any further damage."

(SOURCE: https://www.mimecast.com/blog/top-10-cybersecurity-metrics-and-kpis/)

THE FLAWS WITH THE TRADITIONAL ZERO TRUST FRAMEWORK MODEL

Up to this point in this chapter, we have reviewed the history of the basic Zero Trust Framework model, as well as the Perimeter Defense Model. As it was noted earlier, many businesses are now shying away from this, as it is not the robust tool to be using anymore. Various reasons were also pointed out as well as to how the basic Zero Trust Framework can overcome the shortcomings of the Perimeter Defense model. The various reasons of the former were examined, as well as its strengths and advantages.

Finally, a set of best practices were also reviewed in detail. But believe it or not, despite the basic Zero Trusts Framework "overpowering" the Perimeter Defense model, it still has its own set of shortcomings as well. Thus, at the end of Chapter 4, we proposed our own version of the Zero Trust Framework, which we believe can overcome the weaknesses of the basic one. To summarize, here are weaknesses of it:

1) The use of MFA authentication mechanisms which can still be the target of the Cyberattacker.
2) Having to the end user (or employee) to keep verifying and going through all of the authentication and authorization processes over and over again, each and every time they need access to shared resources.
3) No integrity checks being conducted as authentication information and data is being transmitted to the authorization server, which grants to the end user (or employee) access to the shared resources.
4) Still heavy dependent upon using the password as one of the prime mechanisms for the MFA methodology.

In the remainder of this chapter, we will address each of these shortcomings, and how our proposed Zero Trust Framework can offset these disadvantages as just described. It is important to note at this point that what we propose is still theoretical in nature, and even before it can even be launched into a production environment, it first must be tested. Second, keep in mind that the Zero Trust Framework is designed to work in the internal environment of an organization. It is not all designed to work in the external environment.

The next section will address the first and fourth areas of weaknesses.

THE USE OF BIOMETRICS

We introduced the concept of Biometrics back in Chapter 3. Three separate modalities were examined, which are as follows:

1) Iris Recognition;
2) Fingerprint Recognition;
3) Facial Recognition.

In Chapter 4, we discussed in detail how they can be used as the primary means of both authentication and authorization in the Zero Trust Framework. The three pillars of a successful authentication are:

1) Something you are;
2) Something you have;
3) Something you know.

While this can be achieved in a real-world setting, the truth of the matter is that the second and third forms of authentication can still be easily hacked into. For example, a smart card or an even RSA token can still be intercepted. Although the smart card carries the credentials of the end user (or employee), the data packets can still be intercepted by a malicious third party using a simple network sniffer. FOBs can also be lost or stolen easily, as with RSA tokens.

With the third one, there is still heavy usage of the password, no matter how long or complex that it may be. Even though a password manager can contain all of these passwords, the application can still be hacked into, because even that requires the use of a master password. In the same manner, challenge/response questions can also be tampered with, as the database which contains them can be the target of a brute force or even a dictionary-like attack.

So in the end, the only way an end user (or employee) can positively identify themselves is through the use of Biometrics. This is essentially where a snapshot of either the physiological and/or behavioral characteristics is captured, and the unique features are extracted. So in this regard, we firmly believe that relying exclusively upon the use of Biometric technology is the way to proceed with the Zero Trust Framework. In the end, the goal is to have a passwordless environment for both authentication and authorization, and Biometrics meets the criterion for both sets of circumstances.

But keep in mind that Biometrics may not be suitable for every end user (or employee). For example, they have damage to their finger or even their iris which can be an obstacle in getting an accurate scan. Or they simply may just refuse all together to use any kind of Biometrics, as it would be a total invasion of their privacy rights and civil liberties. So, in these circumstances, a backup or an alternative method must be used.

Biometrics offers a distinct set of advantages over the traditional password, and also any smart card, or token, or FOB. These are as follows:

1) The Biometric Template is nothing but a mathematical file, which represents the image of the physiological and/or behavioral characteristics that were captured. So if for some reason, these templates were to be hijacked by a malicious third party, there is really nothing they can do with it. For example, they cannot take these files and try to use them at a Zero Trust Framework in a different organization, as each Biometric vendor has their own proprietary of processing them. In other words, stealing a Biometric Template is not the same thing as credit card theft.

2) If a Biometric Template were to be stolen, it is very easy to create a new one, in just a matter of a few minutes. There are no calls that are needed to the help desk, and best of all there are administrative costs or overhead with resetting a Biometric Template, unlike the password (where resetting them can be as much as $300-$400/year/employee).

3) Biometric Templates offer a certain degree of non-repudiation. This simply means that the end user (or employee) cannot deny that a specific template is theirs. After all, they have been enrolled by the Biometric system, and the template has been tagged with a unique identifier in the database of the Zero Trust Framework.

4) Biometric Templates can be lost or stolen. The only way that a Cyberattacker can gain access to it is if they rip off the body of the end user (or employee).

5) There is little end user (or employee) training that is required. You just give a demo of the modalities once and that should be enough to complete all of these processes:
   • Enrollment;
   • Verification;
   • Authentication;
   • Verification.

6) Biometrics offers a very high degree of accurate identification, when compared with passwords, challenge/response questions, etc.

Thus, with these compelling reasons, this is why we think that Biometric Technology should be the sole and premier authentication tools for the MFA component for the Zero Trust Framework. We also presented a sequencing model as to which modality should come first, second, and third, in order to provide the most optimal level of MFA. To summarize, it is illustrated below:

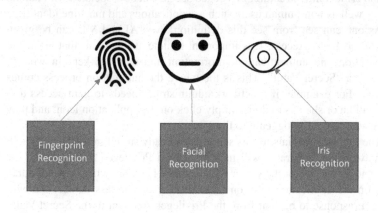

THE WEAKNESS OF REPEATED AUTHORIZATION AND AUTHENTICATION

The second major weakness of the traditional Zero Trust Framework is its repeated need to keep authenticating and authorizing an end user (or an employee) each and every time they need to get access to something. Although the philosophy of the ZTF is to "never trust" but keep verifying, it can really be a nuisance in the end. On top of that, having to go through this process over and over, especially for a larger company, we can use tax computing and processing.

But not only that, the end users (or employees) can also get frustrated with having to go through this process every single time. Is there a solution for this? Yes, and the answer resides in what is known as "Privileged Access Management". In a very broad sense, this area deals with providing a higher level of security for those accounts that are deemed to a higher level than the regular employees. For example, this includes the likes of the CISO, network administrator, database administrator, or even the project manager on a software development team.

Essentially, anybody that has a managerial position at the IT level will have these kinds of account. A technical definition of Privileged Access Management (also known as "PAM") is as follows:

In an enterprise environment, 'privileged access' is a term used to designate special access or abilities above and beyond that of a standard user.

Privileged access allows organizations to secure their infrastructure and applications, run business efficiently and maintain the confidentiality of sensitive data and critical infrastructure. Privileged access can be associated with human users as well as non-human users such as applications and machine identities.

As one can see from see this definition, even AI and ML can be given a Privileged Level Access. It is important to note at this point that all of the authorization and authentication information and data are kept in what is known as a "Secret Vault". This is the where the automation process comes into play. For example, if a network administrator needs to gain access to a server, all he or she has to do is simply click on the application icon, and they will be automatically logged into the server.

The login credentials to this server are already stored in the Secret Vault. The network administrator will have their own Privileged Account, and the rights and privileges for the server will be stored here. So, when this individual clicks on the application icon on their desktop or wireless device, this will trigger a response to be sent from the Privileged Account to the Secret Vault, requesting that access be made in this particular server. From here, the Secret Vault will then transmit the login information to this server, and within seconds, the network administrator will be able to get into the server.

This is illustrated in the diagram below:

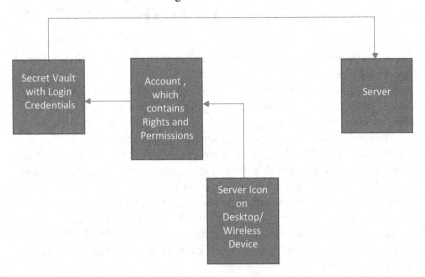

This same approach can also be used for the Biometric Templates, and this will be discussed later in this chapter. But since PAM is such an integral component of our proposed Zero Trust Framework, it is necessary to get a deeper dive into it, in order to gain a much firmer understanding of it. The next few sections will get into more detail.

THE STRAINS OF AN ON PREM PAM

Before the COVID-19 pandemic hit, mostly all businesses had an On Prem Infrastructure, or some parts of it were also located on a Cloud-based platform, such as that of the AWS or Microsoft Azure. But using PAM in this manner is now showing it is not viable for the following reasons:

- The IT and Network Infrastructures of today are no longer deemed to be static in nature. Rather, they are dynamic, with many end users logging in at the same time to access shared resources, as well as the sheer influx of information that businesses have to store today in data warehouses, and the various states that they have to go through. These include if they are archived, being transmitted to different points, or are being processed and analyzed.
- Access to the above often made use of GUIs in order to access a PAM server to get the privileged login information. This was done all manually, thus adding more administrative headaches to an already strained process.
- Logging into separate applications required multiple logins into the PAM server in order to access the proper credentials. Given today's mantra for automation and APIs, and as a result, this is no longer feasible to use.

PAM-based solutions are much better suited for Cloud-based deployments, especially when it comes to the Hybrid Cloud, as the next section examines.

WHY PAM IS BETTER SUITED FOR THE CLOUD

As companies today make the full, 100% move to a Cloud based environment, PAM will be far better suited here for this kind of environment, for the following reasons:

1) Direct access is now a reality
   In today's world, not only do software developers want quick access to their code, but they also now have to follow the rules of DevSecOps. Having a tool such as Active Directory not only provides a secure way to give out privileged access, but the same login credentials can be used over and over again on different development

tools until the so-called "Time To Live" request has expired. In this case, the software developer will then have to go back to Active Directory to get a new set of privileged credentials.

2) You can keep existing workflows

It is a basic fact that humans are sheer creatures of habit. We don't want to change unless we absolutely have to. This is especially true of software developers. Once they have become accustomed to a certain way of creating source code and the tools that are used to compile it; they don't ever want to adopt to a newer way of doing things. But by using PAM in the Cloud, it allows for what is known as "Native Tooling." This allows for the software developers to keep using the tools that they have become accustomed to for so long, while adding in richer layers of authentication protocols.

3) You can make use of the latest code development practices

DevSecOps not totally embraces the automation process, but it also allows PAM to support the following functionalities in the Cloud:

• Promote the usage of infrastructure as a code

This is simply the provisioning and management of your Cloud infrastructure through the use of a certain programming language, rather than using the old fashioned, manual processes. This enhances the speed automation, and helps to cut down on the number of security-related mistakes that occur in the source code creation process.

• Configuration as a code

This allows for an automated version control system to be deployed in your Cloud infrastructure. Through this, you will have increased states of visibility, automated Quality Assurance (QA) testing, and ways to revert back to older editions of the source code, if the need ever arises to do so.

4) It can help to support the various ChatOps tools

The Remote Workforce of today is heavily reliant upon the use of various Instant Messaging (IM) tools now more than ever before. Examples of these include platforms such as Slack and Microsoft Teams. By integrating PAM here, such as Just In Time (JIT) requests allow for privileged access provisioning and approval to happen a lot quicker and more efficiently, than versus doing this on an On Premises infrastructure.

5) It will help to create a passwordless environment

Let's face it, the password has been the de facto standard for both authentication and authorization purposes, and while it is expected to do so, a PAM solution that has been built for the Cloud will help to totally eradicate the need for passwords. This is so because many organizations are now making their best efforts to go to a Passwordless system, such as using tokens, digital certificates, biometrics, etc.

6) It will support diverse kinds of operating environments

Although the movement now is to have PAM support gaining access to administrative credentials that are based in the Cloud (such as that of Azure), a workable solution will also support a Hybrid-like environment where credentials can be granted securely where a company makes use of a Cloud and On Prem environment. This is so because not all companies have chosen yet to make the full migration the Cloud, some still prefer to have part of their infrastructure based on Prem.

THE ADVANTAGES OF USING PAM IN THE CLOUD

Obviously, deploying a PAM-based solution in the Cloud is far better than doing it On Prem. The benefits can be detailed as follows:

1) Centrally store and manage passwords

In today's business world, passwords are among the biggest nemesis that is faced. For example, the cost to reset a password is pegged to be at about $100.00 per employee. If you are a smaller SMB, this may not come to a lot of money in the end. But if you are Fortune 100 company with thousands of employees worldwide dispersed globally, this cost can add up quickly and take a toll on the bottom line. Sure, there are other tools you can use out there, such as the basic Password Manager. But there are inherent security flaws with those as well, especially when it comes to overseeing those employees that have privileged access accounts. What makes PAM unique in this sense is that it brings to the Cloud a high powered "Password Vault", which allows you to manage and assign administrative privileges from a single dashboard in a very safe and secure environment. Nobody else but you will be involved in this process, unless you have other IT Managers that you want to grant this kind of access to.

2) Easier to enforce the concept of least privilege

One of the cardinal rules in Cybersecurity is to give employees just enough access to shared resources for them to do their job on a daily basis. Although this sounds simple in concept, enforcing it and keeping of what employees have is another story. For example, the IT Security team may give out admin-level credentials for a contractor only for the time that they are at your business. Once they are done with their work, this account should be immediately disabled, but many times it gets forgotten about. Or employees may share their passwords behind your back. Whatever the situation is, you need a tool that can oversee and execute the concept of Least Privilege on a real time basis. This is where PAM will play a crucial role. Once deployed in a Cloud environment, it can automatically assign privileges on as needed basis, following the rules and permutations that you have set forth. But best of all, it will terminate those accounts in which no longer need those privileges for certain applications. In other words, you don't have to go from through every computer and wireless device to make sure that the baseline rights and permissions have been assigned and/or deleted. The PAM can store all of the employee profiles, and decide when to allocate and disable permissions automatically. This reduces the risk of forgotten accounts still being activated, which could create a potential backdoor for a Cyberattacker. This is also known as "Just In Time Access" and can even use for members of the IT Security team in order to reduce probability of misuse of admin level privileges.

3) Control remote access

With the COVID-10 pandemic still upon us to varying degrees, the Remote Workforce is here to stay permanently. While many of the initial security issues have been worked out when WFH was first launched a couple of years ago, many of the traditional security tools have been stretched beyond their breaking points. A prime example of this is the VPN. Before the pandemic hit, it did an excellent job of encrypting and securing the network lines of communications. But this was when only 15–20% of all employees were working from home, not the near 100% capacity we are seeing now. Thus, the Cyberattacker now has greater ease in which to penetrate into the VPN, gain access to privileged credentials, and even hijack a remote session. But by implementing a PAM solution into your Cloud environment, you can make use of the Zero Trust Framework and implement what is known as the "Next Generation Firewall", which far surpasses the security thresholds that are offered by the VPN. Not only will this prevent the hijacking of privileged access credentials, but you will have logging activity recorded on a real-time basis, which makes auditing far easier and simpler.

4) Protecting Interconnectedness

As the digital world is coming together, so are the objects that we interact with on a daily basis, which include those in the physical and virtual worlds. This is technically known as the "Internet of Things", or the "IoT". The Cloud has also made it to a great extent these objects to interact with another, but the problem is that the end users still have the security set to the default level, which also includes making use of a very weak password. When PAM is implemented into IoT infrastructure you have deployed into the Cloud, it can manage the creation and assignment of appropriate privileges to the end users on an automatic basis. It will even assign passwords that are far most robust than what a traditional Password Manager can create.

5) Secure DevSecOps in the Cloud

This was a concept that was introduced in the last article. This is a merging of three distinct teams:

- Software development;
- Operations;
- IT Security.

One of the central themes of DevSecOps is automation. While PAM can be used here once to protect privileged access to the source code, it can even do much more than that, for example:

- Secure developer accounts;
- Secure Encryption Keys;
- IT Security.

One of the central themes of DevSecOps is automation. While PAM can be used here once to protect privileged access to the source code, it can even do much more than that, for example:

- Secure developer accounts;
- Secure Encryption Keys;
- Secure Digital Certificates.

A BEST PRACTICES GUIDE FOR DEPLOYING A PAM-BASED SOLUTION

Just deploying the Zero Trust Framework, deploying a PAM-based solution takes careful planning, and testing before releasing it into the Production Environment. Here are a few tips to help ensure a smoother deployment:

1) Understand why you need PAM in the first place

You simply should not deploy a PAM solution just because you think you need to. You first need to think carefully why you need one in the first place, and if you decide to have one, then you need to map it very carefully how it will fit into your IT and Network Infrastructure. You need to fully ascertain which systems, processes, and technologies will be requiring this. Then you need to figure out who will have access to the PAM solution these are keys to the proverbial crown jewels of your organization.

2) Create a PAM password policy

You should already have a password policy in place, but the one for PAM will be different in the sense that you need to craft it so that it addresses the needs of those that have managerial or IT admin titles. By having such a policy in place will help to avoid any misuse of credentials, as Cyberattackers love to go after these kinds of passwords. Therefore, it is recommended that you follow the guidelines from entities as SANS, NIST, and ISO. Remember to change the passwords on a regular basis, and just like for your regular employees, they should be made long and complex and just a little bit more, as these credentials will give access to the most sensitive areas of your business. Also, make sure you implement MFA to make sure 100% that only the legitimate employees have access to privileged accounts. Some of these second and third layers of authentication can include the use of passphrases, RSA tokens, Smart Cards, Biometrics, etc.

3) Change out default passwords

Once you have created a privileged account, make sure that the person to whom it is assigned immediately changes the password. Even though the default password may be long and complex, it is always a good practice to make sure it is changed out when the account it is first activated. Make sure you put into your PAM security policy as to what these passwords need to contain. This will be an alphanumeric string, but to what detail it needs to contain needs to spell out to avoid any confusion or mistakes. Remember, your employees do not have to create these kinds of passwords. The PAM functionality should take care of all of this on an automatic basis. But it is always a clever idea to conduct an audit from time to time as to who has what access when it comes to privileged accounts.

4) Keep tabs as to what is going on

Just as much as the IT Security team has their eye on the Cyber Threat landscape, you also need to keep an eye as to what is happening to the privileged accounts that you assigned. For example, you need to make sure that those employees who have these kinds of accounts are abiding by every letter of the PAM password policy. Of course, you will not be able to keep track of all of this on a 24 X 7 X 365 basis, so this where you can use the tools of both Artificial Intelligence (AI) and Machine Learning (ML). They can keep an eye for you on these accounts on a real-time basis, and alert you in case there is any type of anomalous or suspicious behavior that is transpiring. By keeping track of all this will give you the essential metrics that other members of the C-Suite will ask for, and even the Board of Directors. Keeping track of this will also be very advantageous to you in case you are ever faced with an audit by a regulator from the GDPR, CCPA, HIPAA, etc.

5) Make use of least privilege

This was reviewed in one of the previous articles. With this, you are assigning the minimal number of permissions that are necessary for your employees to conduct their daily job tasks. But this holds true also for those employees that have privileged accounts. Just because they are technically at a higher plane because of the level access, you still need to follow the concept of Least Privilege here as well. For instance, you would grant your IT Security Manager access to all of the devices in your company, so that they can install the needed software patches and upgrades, and perform other troubleshooting tasks. For your Network Administrator, you would assign those rights and permissions that are needed to gain access to the network, the servers, etc. These are privileges that your IT Security Manager would not need, and vice versa.

6) Deletion of temporary accounts

At times, it may be necessary for you to set up a privileged account for an outside third party, especially if you hire a vCISO. Rather than assigning an original, privileged account for them, create a cloned account, and from there, you can then specifically configure the privileged access this individual will need, based upon their contractual obligations to you. Set this account to be inactive on their last day. This way, you will not have to worry about forgetting this task; it will be done automatically for you.

THE MISTAKES THAT ARE MADE WHEN DEPLOYING PAM SOLUTIONS AND HOW TO FIX THEM

Even despite the careful that you and your IT Security take, mistakes are always inevitable. Here is the common list of mistakes made and how to correct them:

1) How up to date are your systems?

The PAM solutions of today are mostly compatible with the latest technologies. For example, deploying a solution for Windows

10 will not work for Windows 8, as it is a much out-of-date system. Before you deploy a PAM configuration, it is very important to make sure that it will work with all of the digital assets in your business. The best way to do this is to take an inventory of all of the hard wired and wireless devices that you have. If anything is outdated, then it is time to discard and upgrade ASAP. This is not just from the standpoint launching PAM, but it is a rule of thumb in Cybersecurity that any outdated device can pose a serious risk, as this this is one of the first items that the Cyberattacker will go after.

2) Not applying passwords properly

This has been a widespread problem for decades, and it is only getting worse. Many employees are given admin passwords, whether it is intentional or not. By doing this, they will be able to login into the most sensitive areas of your business, and cause about any type of havoc, such as data leakages. Or worst yet, they can accidentally give out these passwords to a Cyberattacker in a Social Engineering attack. Password sharing still remains a huge problem as well, and this is one of the leading causes for Insider Attacks to precipitate. To avoid all of these problems, you need to separate out the normal, everyday employees from those who are eligible to have privileged access. The former group should have its own set of security policies, whereas the latter should have its own as well. While both should be enforced equally, the group of employees with the privileged access needs to have further scrutinization. In other words, you don't want to have password misuse here, as the effects can be far more serious. You are dealing with privileged accounts. In order to make sure that all is airtight, it is imperative that you check for any types of suspicious behavior on these types of accounts. This can include multiple login attempts that have failed, or trying to login to a resource to which they have no business in doing so. You can keep a daily watch on all of this by implementing AI tools, and having any alerts or warnings transmitted to the SIEM, where a dedicated member of the IT Security team can proactively tirage them.

3) Create the right kinds of profiles in Active Directory

One of the primary benefits of AD is that you can create as many user groups as you need, and from there, assign privileges on ad hoc basis. For example, you can create a user group for all of the accountants that work in your company, and import into that all of the individual usernames. From there, you can create all of the privileges for that profile, and deploy of all of the privileges and permissions in a simultaneous fashion. While this is certainly advantageous, it can also prove to be a serious mistake from the standpoint of the privileged user groups. You do not want a help desk specialist to have network administration privileges assigned to them by accident. So, in this manner, you are probably better off assigning rights and privileges to privileged accounts manually, rather than on an ad hoc basis. True, this will take more time, but at least you will have confidence that the appropriate permissions have been applied. This is where having a separate list created for the privileged accounts will be very useful, as described earlier in this article.

4) The move to the Cloud

The movement to the Cloud is now happening at a pace than it was ever imagined. A lot of this has been fueled by the COVID-19 pandemic, and in this rush, security is now a forgotten about topic here. When you move all of your applications to the Cloud, you need to take an inventory of what you have just moved, and from there, determine which of those assets need the highest level of protection. Of course, you will need some sort of PAM architecture here, but this too will need to protect as well. In other words, you simply cannot assign privileged accounts and merely trust your IT Security team will not run off with them. There could be a malicious threat actor here as well. Therefore, you will even need to keep a careful eye here, because in today's world, you simply cannot trust anybody anymore, even those employees that have been around for a long time. In other words, the days of having implicit trust even in the most minute degree are now over; it is time for the Zero Trust Framework.

5) Outside vendors

As the world becomes more interconnected partly fueled by the Internet of Things (IoT) revolution, businesses are becoming more dependent now upon hiring third-party contractors to help meet customer demands and expectations. It is highly recommended these days that you have a deep vetting process in place before you make a selection. But this is where most companies make their mistake. They don't continually monitor the hired third party after the fact. It is very important that you do audits on a regular basis, in order to confirm that there are no leakages of your datasets, and that all privileged accounts that have been assigned are not being misused in any way.

THE IMPORTANCE OF JUST IN TIME (JIT) ACCESS

In the world of supply chain management, there is a concept known as "Just In Time Inventory". This is when the raw inputs are delivered to the manufacturer right before they are needed to complete the final product. The idea here is to eliminate excess inventory in an effort to cut unnecessary costs. This is also somewhat similar to JIT Access, but instead, it deals with the establishment of the rights, privileges, and permissions that are needed in a privileged account, and is assigned to a specific role right when it is needed the most.

To illustrate this example, take the role of the Project Manager that is overseeing a software development team. This group is developing a web-based application for a client, and the Project Manager needs to gain superuser network access in order to see how the prototype product will work on both the front and back ends of a server.

To accomplish, the IT Security team will provide JIT Access that is designed specifically for the role of a Network Administrator. During this time, the Project Manager will then see how the protype runs and make any notes of tweaks and adjustments that need to be made to the source code. Once this task is over, the IT Security team will then completely disable the JIT Access until it is needed again for a similar situation.

This example illustrates what JIT Access is, and from the standpoint of a specific role. In a company, there can be accounts that are established for specific privileged roles, with all of the rights and permissions that go with them. So, when it is absolutely needed, it can be activated, and once the work is done, it can be disabled, or deactivated once again.

The basic idea of JIT Access is to avoid keeping privileged access accounts in an always "on mode", which can be a huge risk from the standpoint of Cybersecurity. It is also based upon the principle of "Least Privilege", which states that only the minimal rights and permissions should be given, even in the case of super user accounts, like PAM.

The Types of JIT Access Accounts

There are a number of role-based JIT accounts that can be created, and some of them are as follows:

1) Justification-based access
   This can also be referred to technically as the "broker and remove" accounts. For example, if the Project Manager needs to have Network

Admin privileges, they have to provide written justification to the manager of the IT Security team why this kind of access is needed and for how long. Once this is deemed to be satisfactory enough, the Project Manager is then given this type of role-based access once it is needed, and will terminate immediately once the work is done. The written justification must also include the tasks that will be done, and anything that is done outside of these bounds will be red flagged as suspicious behavior, and thus, the Project Manager will be stripped of this super user access immediately. It is important to note here that the login credentials in these JIT Accounts are locked in a separate vault, and remain unknown to most people in the organization.

2) Ephemeral accounts

In this situation, JIT access is given to complete just one specific task. For example, if you bring in a third-party contractor to deploy a certain piece of software en masse to your employees wireless device, then you will be giving them this only this of kind of access. Once the work is done, this account will then be deleted by the IT Security team.

3) Privilege escalation

This kind of JIT Access is used for your longer time employees, typically the direct hire ones. Going back once again to the example of the Project Manager, if he or she needs only a subset of the Network Administrator rights and privileges to complete just a few tasks, then you can add these permissions into their existing PAM account. Then once the Project Manager is done completing their tasks, these elevated permissions can be quickly removed from their existing PAM account. One of the advantages to this is that there is no need to waste time switching complete accounts over, and flipping them back later, which can cause a security risk.

The Benefits of JIT Access

There are numerous strategic advantages to using this kind of approach, some of which are as follows:

1) The level of Cybersecurity is improved

When employees are given just what they need to access shared resources at the most minimal level possible, your Cybersecurity posture will be greatly strengthened. There are no lingering privileged accounts out there that the Cyberattacker can take advantage of, and by taking this kind of approach, your attack surface also decreases.

2) The assignment of accounts can be automated
   JIT Access can be provisioned on an automatic basis, thus eliminating paperwork and the time it takes to grant formal approval.

3) It can be applied to other areas
   JIT Access can be flexible as well, and it is not a rigid methodology. For example, software developers can be given JIT Access in order of module templates, which supports the workflows of the DevOps team. This is crucial when it is time to create software builds and QA and test them. The concept of JIT Access can be applied to other departments in your organization as well. For example, if the Finance team needs to have access to employee salaries, JIT Access can be used so that they can retrieve this data from the Human Resources department for the time period that is needed.

4) Easier management of third parties
   Whenever an outside contractor is hired, there is always some fear that they might be given more access than what is needed. But by using JIT Access, this problem is negligible, especially if you are using Ephemeral-based accounts.

THE FOUR PILLARS TO PAM SUCCESS

The top four major components that the CISO and his or her IT Security team need to examine are as follows:

1) Track every account
   A privileged account is one which has some super user privileges to a certain degree. These credentials could involve things such as database administration, network administration, security administration, etc. Therefore, these kinds of accounts need to be safeguarded very carefully, and constantly monitored. After all, if a Cyberattacker can gain access to just one on Privileged Account, then the chances are much greater that they will be able to move laterally in a quick manner to your digital assets. Therefore, any good PAM solution should have functionality to keep track of each and every account that has been, even if it is for just a few hours. Also, the solution must be capable to either delete or deprovision any inactive PAM-based accounts. Also, information about the use of Privileged Accounts needs to be collected, which will form your governance strategy as to how they will be given out into the future.

2) The limiting of access control

There are two characteristics of Privileged Accounts that you need to be aware of: 1) Access Control; and 2) Access Governance. With the former, you need to keep track of all of the changes that are made from the Privileged Accounts itself. For example, these accounts can be regarded to be dynamic in nature. The profiles and the groups in these accounts will change over time, depending largely on how the security policy of your organization changes. Thus, the IT Security team must keep track of these changes. If there are too many of them being made from the established baseline, then this could be a cause for concern. With the latter, you need to keep track of what Privileged Accounts can access what. You do not want any crossover between the entitlements that have been established for a network administrator to have database privileges. In other words, a Privileged Account should only give access to what is urgently needed for just a brief period of time.

3) Record activity

Any good PAM-based solution must give the CISO and the IT Security team the ability to capture the activity of all of the Privileged Accounts on a real-time basis. The reason for this is that this data will prove to be extremely valuable when it comes down to doing an internal audit, or even one that may be conducted by federal regulators. However, parsing through all of this data can be a very burdensome task, and can even prove to be an administrative nightmare. Thus, the PAM-based solution must have the ability to give a visual representation to all of the information that is being collected. Moreover, it should also have the functionality for the IT Security team to build specific queries not only to extract data, but to also examine what if scenarios down the road.

4) Automation

In today's world, the IT Security team is inundated by threat vectors on a minute-by-minute basis. Although constantly Privileged Accounts is of a high a priority, it cannot be done by a human being; it is just too much to ask for. Therefore, any PAM-based solution must have automation built into for the following, to just name a few:

• Doing mundane and repeatable tasks;
• Establishing configuration changes;
• Conducting software upgrades and patch maintenance;
• Service shutdowns and startups;
• Event log management;
• The establishment of MFA.

THE FINER POINTS OF PRIVILEGED ACCESS MANAGEMENT

As you deploy the Zero Trust Framework for your organization, keep these granular details in mind as well:

1) Privileged access governance

   We all know that most organizations have higher level accounts than from the rest of the employee base. These are the Privileged Accounts, and these are typically assigned to those employees who have some sort of administrative role, such as a network or even a database manager. Even a project manager on a web development project could very well be assigned a privileged account so that they can oversee the project from the beginning to end. Although the goal of a PAM-based solution is to properly govern these accounts when they are needed and not needed, they do not observe how the privileged end user actually interacts with the sensitive data to which they have been access to. For example, are there any malicious activities that are transpiring? Are these privileged accounts being abused in any way. This is where the Privileged Access Governance component comes into play. From this, in a single view, you can see any signs of abnormal behavior toward the data. There are log files that are provided for this very reason, so you will be able to get any first indicators of an insider attack that could be brewing. This comes all under the umbrella of what is known as "User Behavior Analysis". The Privileged Access Governance functionality can also draw out various visual diagrams as to where all of your sensitive datasets reside at. This is especially useful to have in order to come into compliance with various data privacy laws.

2) PAM discovery

   If the organization is especially large (starting at a 1000-employee size or greater), Privileged Accounts can be created and used without even the IT Security team knowing about it. The primary reason for this is that it is the job of the IT department to do all of this. Very often, there is a lack of communication between both parties, and quite often, one party does know what the other is doing (and vice versa). Therefore, you need some sort of functionality in your PAM-based solution to keep of any Privileged Accounts that are being created and onboarded. This is where the PAM Discovery component will come into use. Scans can be triggered automatically and messages sent to the IT Security team whenever a brand-new Privileged Account has been initiated and onboarded. This functionality will also give you the ability to keep a continuous eye on those Privileged Accounts and recycle those that are outdated into a newer state with updated rights, privileges, and permissions.

3) Privileged credential management

This is can also be referred to as "Privileged Password Management". However, this is not to be confused with that of a Password Manager. This refers to just the creation and storage of passwords for the everyday consumer, who has many passwords to remember. The Privileged Credential Management component of a PAM-based solution keeps track of those login credentials that are strictly associated with Privileged Accounts. Technically, it can be specifically defined as follows:

It is the secure storing, sharing, creating, and handling of privileged passwords. Privileged password management may alternatively be referred to as privileged credential management, enterprise password management, enterprise password management, enterprise password security. Privileged passwords are a subset of credentials that provide elevated access and permissions across accounts, applications, and systems.

(SOURCE: https://www.beyondtrust.com/resources/glossary/ privileged-password-management)

As can be seen from the definition above, privileged passwords are just one part of all of the passwords that are established for all of the other employees of a company. But it is considered to be a subset, given the special characteristics that they have. But passwords are only a set of credentials that can be used with PAM-based solutions. These include tokens, SSH keys, etc.

Because of the sensitivity that is involved with credentials associated with PAM accounts, they have to be monitored in a much different way than other password management techniques. In this regard, some of the best practices include the following:

- Keeping a constant eye on these kinds of credentials;
- On a 110% level, privileged credentials must be rotated on a regular basis as per the security policies that have been established;
- Bring all of the privileged credentials into one central location, which is known as the "Vault";
- Keep an on malicious behavior that can impact any PAM-based credential. This should be an automated basis, which will most likely make use of AI and ML plugins to comb through all of the log files.

4) Privileged session management

This component of a PAM-based solution is meant to serve as a system of checks and balances. For example, if a network administrator logs in using a Privileged Account, then he or she can be observed on a real-time basis by the IT Security team from the moment they log in, when they are in session, and when they log out. The primary objective here is that somebody else with the same privileges can keep an audit trail by another person who also has the same types and kinds of privileges. This can also serve to be very advantageous for compliance reasons.

In Chapter 4, we presented an initial model of our proposed Zero Trust Framework model, toward the end. In this chapter, we have broken down that model, and discussed thus far, how it can overcome three of the weaknesses of the basic Zero Trust Framework model. So, it is now important to review to how the concepts of PAM will fit into our proposed model. This is what we have so far:

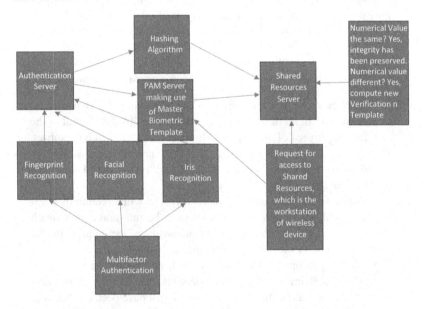

To summarize the key steps:

1) The end user (or the employee) requests access to the shared resources, by clicking on the appropriate icon.
2) This is then transmitted as a message to the PAM Server, which then pings the Authentication Server to send over the Master Biometric

Template to the Shared Resources Server. Note that in Chapter 4 this was referred to as the "New Verification Template", which is a combination of the Fingerprint, Facial, and Iris Recognition Templates.

3) Authentication to the Shared Resources Server happens in just a few seconds.

Thus, as one can see from the diagram above, the repeated authentication and authorization are no longer needed in our proposed Zero Trust Model.

The next thing you will notice is the use of Hashing Algorithms. This is to ensure that the Master Biometric Template remains intact on the route from the Authentication Server to the Shared Resources Server. But even here, Hashing Algorithms are prone to Cyberattacks as well, and will be addressed in the next section. Also, this model as depicted will be updated in the next section as well, which will present the final one. In it, we discuss how the Quantum Mechanics, BioCryptography, Public Key Infrastructure, and various other mechanisms will come into play.

THE USE OF QUANTUM MECHANICS IN OUR PROPOSED MODEL OF THE ZERO TRUST FRAMEWORK

We have now approached this phase of the book where we discuss how the concepts of Quantum Mechanics could possibly fit into our proposed Zero Trust Model. But it has been mentioned before, Quantum Mechanics is still very much a theoretical field in the work of physics, so what we propose in this part of chapter is strictly theoretical. But, we do believe that as research and technology continue to evolve over time, it could become a reality one day.

But before delve any further, it is first important to provide a definition of what Quantum Mechanics is all about. Technically, it is defined as follows:

> Quantum Mechanics is the study of very small things. More specifically, it's the study of how matter and energy interact on the scale of atomic and sub-atomic particles.
>
> *(SOURCE: https://revolutionized.com/quantum-mechanics-101/)*

In a small way, it can be likened to that of the Internet of Things (IoT). In this instance, there is the study of how things interact with each other in both the physical worlds. But the difference here is that we can actually see and even hold some of these objects in our very own hands. But with Quantum Mechanics, these objects are at the atomic and/or the subatomic level. This area has a number of key properties that are associated with it, and they are as follows:

1) Positioning

   The position and the motion of a particle are mathematically indeterminate. But if for some reason you can figure out the momentum, it will be that much more difficult to compute the location of it.

2) Quantization

   Objects in the world of Quantum Mechanics have only discrete, mathematical values that are associated with it. If any of the characteristics of these objects change, they do not so in a gradual manner. The values with them change in a "hard" manner, without taking a slower, more measured approach.

3) Tiny particles

   Matter is composed of electrons, protons, and neutrons. It is also composed of light, and the particles that are associated with that are known as "Photons", which will be reviewed later.

4) Quantum entanglement

   This is concept where it demonstrates what is known as "non-locality". It means that the particles are on a mathematical level, permanently correlated with one another. Although these particles are quite far apart from one another, any effect on one will have an immediate effect on the remaining particles.

Finally, there is an area of Quantum Mechanics that is fast emerging beyond the realms of just theory. It is known as "Quantum Computing". This makes use of uncertainty and the latest principles of data science to come up with a newer and faster way to store what is known as "Bog Data". These datasets are broken into "Quantum Bits", or "Qubits", and are considered to be either in of two states: on or off.

QUANTUM CRYPTOGRAPHY

A subset field of Quantum Mechanics is what is known as "Quantum Cryptography". As you can see, Cryptography plays a huge part in our proposed Zero Trust Framework model. But a specific area of this is known as the "Quantum Key Distribution". A technical definition of it as follows:

> The process of using quantum communication to establish a shared key between two trusted parties so that an untrusted eavesdropper cannot learn anything about that key.
>
> (SOURCE: https://sectigo.com/resource-library/quantum-cryptography).

In the model that we proposed at the very end of Chapter 4, there was an illustration of the Key Distribution Center (also known as the "KDC"). This acts as a tool in which the digital certificates (which are also known as the public and private keys) could be created and issued in an efficient manner to both the Authentication Server and the Shared Resources Server. In fact, there was even a review of it as well. But despite all of the safeguards that have been taken to help protect it, it can still be prone to a Cyberattack.

Therefore, we will play very close attention to the KDC in this part of the Chapter. So far, we have corrected three of the four major weaknesses of the basic Zero Trust Framework, which are as follows:

1) Using Biometric Technology as the sole means for MFA;
2) Getting rid of the repeated need for verification;
3) Eliminating the need for the password in its entirety (again, by making use of Biometric Technology).

There is one more flaw that still remains, and that is providing a more robust way for the integrity checks of the Master Biometric Template, as it gets transmitted from the Authentication Server to the Shared Resources Server. We have pointed out in Chapter 4 that Hashing Algorithms can be used, but they have their own security flaws as well (this is where the use of Photons would come into play.

So in the end, there are three parts left before our proposed Zero Trust Framework Model can be considered to be complete, at least on a theoretical basis:

1) Adding further levels of protection to the Public Key Infrastructure;
2) Using the Quantum Key Distribution Center;
3) Making use of the Photon Particle Structures.

Once all of this has been reviewed, we will then provide an illustration of all of this. But before we go into any further detail, we believe that a formal review of the literature of what we are proposing should also be included.

This is the topic of the next section.

THE LITERATURE REVIEW

One of the more powerful and recent research studies of the Quantum Key Distribution Center was conducted by Ram Kumar Jayaraman and Manoj Kumar. Their work was entitled "Quantum Cryptography and Quantum Key Distribution".

The basis for their theoretical work states that the digital certificates (the Public Key and the Private Key) are distributed between two endpoints (in our proposed model of the Zero Trust Framework, this would be the Authentication Server and the Shared Resources Server) using a series of photon-based particles. There are four major components here for Quantum Key Distribution, and they are as follows:

1) The Heisenberg uncertainty principle

   A scientist, known as W. Heisenberg, ran a series of experiments in order to accurately gauge the mathematical position of any electron, by making use of a gamma ray microscope. While the location of electron can be accurately determined, the others cannot be measured, because it would disrupt the entire quantum-based system. As it relates to our proposed Zero Trust Framework, a private key can be sent from the Authentication Server to the Shared Resources Server, which can be done by making use of a single photon. The advantage here is that a Cyberattacker can maliciously intercept a photon in transit without disturbing the integrity of the states of the other photons. Thus, this provides another unique to positively identify the specific threat variant which has been launched.

2) The quantum entanglement

   This is where a single photon can be split off into two separate ones, by making use of a laser beam. This causes the two photons to be entangled from within each other, and while the property of one photon could potentially be measured, the other cannot be quantitatively determined. This could be another advantageous way to protect the integrity of the Master Biometric Template. In other words, while it could be possible for a Cyberattacker to intercept one photon, there is nothing that they can do to the other photon, as its location will not be known. This is illustrated in the diagram below:

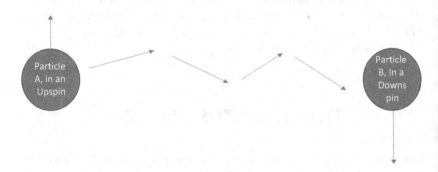

3) Photon polarization

This can be viewed as a two-state quantum system. For example, it consists of rectilinear polarization basis and a diagonal polarization basis. With the former, the structure of the photons can be represented with either a 0-degree (horizontal) or 90-degree (vertical) quantum state. With the latter, it can be represented with 45-degree or 135-degree direction. The polarization of a photon is known only at the time of actual measurement. It plays a major role in preventing integrity issues in communications, where eavesdropping attacks are common. This is illustrated in the diagram below:

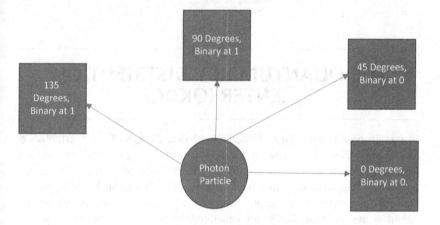

4) Quantum no-cloning

This is where an unknown quantum state cannot be cloned, thus it is called a "No-Cloning Theorem". In this kind of instance, a Cyberattacker cannot modify the information and data that is being transmitted between a sender and a receiver; in other words, there is no further amplification that is involved.

5) The Ekert's protocol

This is where the concept of photon entanglement comes into play. The photon's source is created by either the sender (the Authentication Server) or the receiver (the Shared Resources Sever). The source transmits entangled pairs of photons. The photons are entangled because the directions in which they are spinning are not known. This is yet another effective way to ensure the integrity of the Master Biometric Template, as it makes its way across the two servers. This is illustrated in the diagram below:

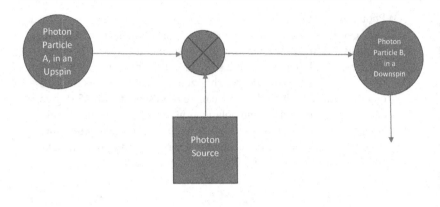

THE QUANTUM KEY DISTRIBUTION CENTER (QKDC)

In our proposed Zero Trust Framework Model, the QKDC will establish a shared private session between the Authentication Server and the Shared Resources Server by making use of a series of photons to transmit Master Biometric Template over the optical fiber cable. This is all based upon the Heisenberg uncertainty principle, as described previously in this chapter. In summary, it states that photons are generated randomly in one of the two polarized quantum states. Further, the property of a photon cannot be computed without altering the information in the photon itself.

As long as the photons remain in an unaltered state, then the integrity of the Master Biometric Template can be assured. But, if there is a change in state of even a single photon in the array structure, then the Authentication Server and Shared Resources Server will know that the Master Biometric Template has been compromised and cannot be trusted.

It is important to keep in mind at this point that the QKDC can support three types of certificates, which are as follows, and they all still live up to the standards of the X.509 protocol:

1) Quantum safe certificates
   These make use of quantum encryption algorithms, pending approval by the National Institute of Standards and Technology (NIST).
2) Hybrid certificates
   These kinds of certificates contain a traditional RSA key and signature, as well as quantum-based key and signature. This type of

certificate for an organization to get prepared for a full migration to a Zero Trust Framework that makes use of Quantum Mechanics.

3) Composite quantum - safe certificates

These kinds of certificates are close to Hybrid Certificates because they contain a series of keys and signatures, but are different in the sense that they use a combination of existing and quantum-safe encryption algorithms.

As it was stated numerous times throughout this book, you simply cannot migrate to a Zero Trust Framework in fell swoop, especially if it makes use of the concepts of Quantum Mechanics. It is always best to use a phased in approach, and here are some guidelines in doing that:

- Make sure that the Public Key Infrastructure (PKI) you are using can support the QKDC. Most PKIs of today have some sort of key infrastructure, but they must support quantum certificates.
- The Authentication and the Shared Resources Server must also be updated in order to support both quantum-based certificates and the photon particle array structures.
- Confirm that the applications which are stored in the Shared Resources Server are updated so that they can also support the use of quantum certificates and photon particle array structures.
- Every PKI has what is known as a "Root Store". This contains all of the digital certificates that are considered to be at the root level. But, when making the move to a Zero Trust Framework based on Quantum Mechanics, this Root Store has to be upgraded as well so that it can handle the quantum-based certificates.
- Make sure to get rid of all of the old digital certificates, especially the RSA-based ones.

THE PHOTON PARTICLE ARRAY STRUCTURES

As it was reviewed in Chapter 4, it is the Hashing Algorithm that is primarily used in PKIs today in order to confirm the integrity of a message that was sent from the point of origin to the point of destination, and vice versa. Essentially, by using this kind of technique, a numerical value called a "Hash" is computed. If this number stays the same from Point A to Point B (and also vice versa), then one can confirm that integrity of the message has been intact, and it has not been altered in any way in transit.

But, the Hashing Algorithm is prone to Cyberattacks as well; therefore, in our proposed Zero Trust Framework, we make use of the Photon Particles as a replacement for the Hashing Algorithm. In this regard, we propose an Array Structure of at least two Photon Particles. This can be constructed by using any of the theoretical frameworks discussed earlier in this chapter. For example:

1) With the Heisenberg uncertainty principle
   If one Photon Particle is hijacked by the Cyberattacker, then the integrity of the other will still remain intact.
2) With the quantum entanglement
   If one Photon Particle is maliciously captured, the location of the other will be indeterminate.
3) With photon polarization
   The vector orientations of both Photon Particles will remain unknown, thus making this one of the strongest options to use.
4) With quantum no-cloning
   Under this scenario, both Photon Particles cannot be cloned, making this a very secure option as well.
5) With the Eckert's protocol
   In this scenario, the two Photon Particles are spinning in an unknown rotation, which can be very difficult for the Cyberattacker to accurately quantify. This is also yet another strong and viable option to use.

The primary reason for choosing a two-photon Particle Array Structure is that if one Photon were to be maliciously intercepted, the second will act as a form of redundancy, thus ensuring the continued integrity of the Master Biometric Template.

OUR PROPOSED ZERO TRUST FRAMEWORK MODEL

Finally, taking into account the updates made to remediate the flaws of the Basic Zero Trust Framework Model, our model now looks like this:

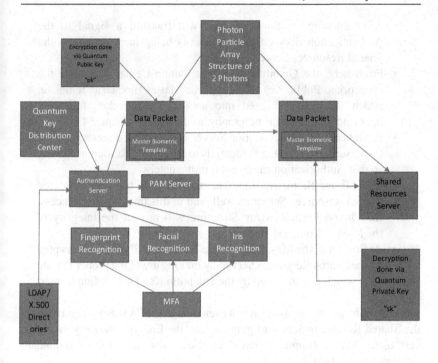

Here is a detailed description of how our proposed Zero Trust Framework Model works:

1) The end user (or employee) first gets enrolled into the Authentication Server by completing the Enrollment Process. This means going through each of the Biometric Modalities as depicted above. At this stage, the Enrollment Template is created, and is stored permanently in the LDAP/X.500 Directory Databases.

2) They then go through the Verification Process, which is the same as the Enrollment Process. From here, the Verification Template is created.

3) At this point, the Enrollment and the Verification Templates are created to form what is known as the "Master Biometric Template". The two are first matched, and a successful match is recorded into the PAM Server. The Master Biometric Template is also stored in the LDAP/X.500 Directories.

4) Suppose now the end user (or the employee) wishes to gain access to the Shared Resources Server. All they have to do is click on the appropriate icon onto their device. This will then trigger the following process to occur:

- After clicking on the icon, this will transmit a signal to the Authentication Server that a request is being made to access the Shared Resources Server.
- From here, the Quantum Key Distribution Center will issue the appropriate Public Key to encrypt the Master Biometric Template, which is already encased into another Data Packet, following the principles of Biocryptography, as detailed in Chapter 4.
- From here, the Authentication Server will transmit a message to the PAM Server to send the credentials to the Shared Resources Server, so that Authorization can happen immediately.
- The Master Biometric Template will also be transmitted to the Shared Resources Server as well, and in this transmission process, the Photon Particle Array Structure will protect the integrity of the Master Biometric Template.
- At this point, the Master Biometric Template will also be decrypted by the Shared Resources Server, by making use of the proper Private Key, which is also issued by the Quantum Key Distribution Center.

It is important to note at this point that even though the PAM Server can instruct the Shared Resources Server to grant access, the Encryption/Decryption process of the Master Biometric Template also serves as another or redundant Authentication check.

Threat Modeling/ Threat Hunting

5

So far in this book, we have covered a lot of concepts about the Zero Trust Framework and the components that go into. But it is important to keep in mind that this is a methodology that is designed to work primarily for the internal environment of your business, not the external environment. You can segment out your internal IT and Network environments, but not anything outside of it.

Even despite the resiliency of the Zero Trust Framework, it too can be prone to Cyberattacks and hacks. Therefore, you need to protect this environment, with the tools of both Threat Hunting and Threat Modeling.

It is also important to keep in mind that Threat Modeling also makes use of modern tools as well to predict the future Cyber Threat Landscape. In this regard, the use of Artificial Intelligence (AI) and Machine Learning (ML) are great boons to the Threat Modeler.

WHAT EXACTLY IS THREAT MODELING?

In broad terms, it is the process of looking and evaluating the risks that your company faces (of course, you will only know this after you have conducted an independent Risk Assessment Analysis), as well as any other threats, and vulnerabilities that are known at that point in time.

From here, the statistical probabilities are mapped out on the chances of being hit, and your ability to mitigate those beforehand.

It is important to keep in mind that with Threat Modeling you are taking a holistic view of your environment, you are not just simply examining a group of digital assets and the appropriate controls that go with them. With Threat

Modeling, you are taking every bit of intelligence that you have, whether they are log files or even reports outputted by your SIEM, and trying to come up with the best to beef up your lines of defenses.

THE PROCESS INVOLVED IN THREAT MODELING

There are typically four steps that are involved, and they include the following:

1) Deciding upon the framework:

   Threat Modeling is also viewed as a science, and as such, it is imperative that you make use of some sort of methodology in order to yield the maximum results from it. In this regard, probably the two most popular frameworks that can be used are the Cyber Kill Chain from Lockheed Martin (which can be seen here) and the OWASP (which can be seen here). With this approach, you will be examining those parts of the environment that you want to take a closer look at, in terms of where they stand right now in terms of their security level.

2) Identification:

   In this second step, you will take an inventory of those threats vectors, both that are known and predicted, and examining the kind of damage they could potentially cause. Keep in mind that these are what if scenarios, and because of that, you should consider making equal use of AI and ML tools to help your IT Security come up with each and every possibility that you can. However, you should also make use of your team's experience as well to come up with scenarios.

3) Mitigation:

   At this stage, after you have carefully mapped out what could potentially go wrong, you and your IT Security team need to come up with a plan as to how these variants, should they impact, your business can be remediated as quickly as possible. This is where the Incident Response (IR) Plan and the Disaster Recovery (DR) Plan will become especially important. These plans should be detailed enough so that they can be used for any kind of attack, not just a particular one. After all in the end, once a breach has occurred, getting back up and running ASAP will be crucial, and you simply will not have the time to find the right one to use. In other words, these plans should take the proverbial "one size fits all approach". This part of the Threat Modeling phase will also give you the time to also take an inventory of all of the security tools and technologies that you have in place, and try to consolidate them as much as possible. For example, suppose you have ten firewalls at certain locations in your IT/Network Infrastructure. The question you need to be asking and answering is how can we strategically place them so that only the minimal is needed. For instance, how can we make use of instead of three firewalls? This way of thinking will not only help to reduce your attack surface, but will also help your IT Security analyze the log files for investigative purposes after the breach has been stopped.

4) Remediation:

This last phase of Threat Modeling can be considered the simplest, but it will require the teamwork of all of the employees in your company. This is the actual dress rehearsal of the both the IR and DR plans. They will address two key concerns:

- How quickly a threat variant can be mitigated;
- How quickly you can bring back up your mission critical processes and operations.

The rehearsing of these plans is not a one-time deal, but rather, they should be practiced on a regular basis, preferably at least once a quarter. Also, pieces of documentation should be updated as quickly with any refinements or enhancements that are needed.

MAKING THE CASE FOR THREAT MODELING

To the Software Development Team

As it was described earlier in this chapter, Threat Modeling is still almost a brand new field in its own right. You simply don't see a lot of people being directly by it, like you would see Pen Testing. So, if Threat Modeling does not exist at your organization, you the vCISO or CISO, are going to have to do a really good job in making the case why you need to hire some talent in this regard. You will probably get a lot pushback initially, from within different groups in your organization.

First of course will be software development teams. These people literally live in their own islands, and there is a lot of pressure now to bring the out into the limelight into the world of Cybersecurity. The primary reason for this is that they were never held accountable for any security risks in the source code that they wrote for the Web applications they were creating for the client.

But now, with the advent of open source software being used much more now, there are also open sourced APIs that are being used. Many times, these APIs are not tested or upgraded with the latest software patches and upgrades, thus causing more risks in the source code that is being developed. This is a whole new for software developers to face, and there is a lot of resistance to it. Not to mention, there is also a strong move in Corporate America to create a new team called "DevSecOps". The attempt here is to bring in the software development, IT security, and operations from within a company to act as double and even a triple check to the source code that is being developed.

So, now you throw into the mix Threat Modelers who also have to work with the software development team. The primary reason for this is that the Threat Modeler needs to know where the initial vulnerabilities are at so that they can make predictions as to how future threat variants can penetrate into them. Of course, software developers don't want to know this even more than what they already have heard.

Another primary reason why your software development team will have a fierce opposition to any Threat Modeler coming on board to your organization is that they will simply view as them as an extra layer of red tape that they need to go through. In the world of software development, this is technically known as "You Ain't Gonna Need It", also known as "YAGNI". As a vCISO or CISO, this is going to be a tricky situation to handle. Of course, you could just put the hammer down and say, "This is the way it is going to be", or you could try to get them to adopt to the idea of working with a Threat Modeler just as much as they have to work with a DevSecOps team.

From Upper Management

With this group of people, it is not the C-Suite, but rather, it is that group of people in your organization that hold some sort of managerial title, and they supervise a team of other individuals that work underneath them. A typical example of this is the IT Security Manager. Of course, as vCISO or CISO, you have the ultimate to basically them they need to accept the fact that a new Threat Modeler is coming on board into the team, and that will have to supervise them whether they like it or not. But of course, this is not the ideal situation to take either.

So in this particular situation, you need to come up with some sort of plan that fully explains the need for a Threat Modeler on the IT Security team. This does not have to be a 200-page report, but rather just a few pages summarizing the need for such a title in your organization. Probably, the biggest case you can make here is that after all, if you Pen Testing teams and Threat Hunting teams, why not have a person that can take all of this intelligence and information/data that was collected in the reconnaissance phase and use that to help predict what the future can hold?

Of course, they will counter this argument by stating the fact that Artificial Intelligence and Machine Learning tools exist that can do a lot of this already, so why go into the extra expense of hiring somebody? Well, as the vCISO or CISO, your counter will be much stronger: AI and MIL are just tools of technology, and are prone to make some serious mistakes. You also need that human eye to go over the outputs that they have created in order to make sure that any predictions for the Cyber well-being of your company are both sound and reasonable.

From the Project Management Team

As it was earlier stated in this chapter, ultimately, your Threat Modeler (or perhaps even Threat Modeling team) will have to work with a much larger group of people, other than your software development team. This is the going to be the Project Team that has been assigned a certain development project, such as that of creating major Web application for an online store merchant. So, if you want to Threat Modeler to play an integral part in this you have to have the answers to the following questions already in for the Project Manager to review. Examples of these include the following:

- How will the Threat Modeler be involved with the Project Management team?
- What kinds of tasks will they do?
- How will they assist in the software development process?
- What kind of preparatory work will he or she need to do before each sprint or milestone which is to be completed in this project?
- What further resources will be available to the Threat Modeler from the Project Management team should they require it?
- If there are serious disagreements that arise from the Threat Modeler and the Project Management team, how will they be resolved?
- What are the expected deliverables of the Threat Modeler to the Project Management team?
- How will the Threat Modeler participate in the process of deliverables?
- How will interaction take place between the Threat Modeler and others? (For example, will it be face to face, emails, video conferencing, etc.?)
- What are the documents that the Threat Modeler will have to produce?
- Who will have ultimate ownership and responsibility for these particular documents?
- What are the specific documents that will be needed?
- What will the naming and versioning conventions be for those documents?

- Where will these documents live, and how will they be secured? (e.g., using Blockchain-based technologies)?

Remember in the end, your Threat Modeler or Threat Modeling team is just one component of your Project Management team and your overall IT Security strategy. For example, when it comes to the former, their role is to almost a devil's advocate. For all of the weaknesses and gaps that have been found (even after they have been remediated), the Threat Modeler needs to pose serious challenges to see how well the newly built application can counter effectively future Cyber Threats, based on the intel and information/data that they already have on hand.

Finally, the Threat Modeling and Project Management Dichotomy are illustrated below:

HOW TO HAVE QUALITY-BASED THREAT MODELING MEETINGS

It is very important to keep in mind that Threat Modelers are also human beings, and while a lot of the intel they need to conduct their research comes from already collected information and data, a lot of knowledge can be shared also with other members in the IT Security team. In fact, many businesses across Corporate America have been heavily criticized for the lack of team communications between the IT Security team and the CISO, and even the vCISO and CISO.

So therefore in this subsection of this chapter, we take a critical look at this aspect as you foster and continue to grow your Threat Modeling team.

The Composition of the Team Meetings

Of course, anybody can have a meeting for the sake of having one. But when it comes to Cybersecurity especially, time is extremely valuable, and you should really only schedule meetings with all members of your IT Security team when needed. But for illustrative purposes, let us go back to the example of the Project Management that was reviewed in detail. To have a really good meeting that will be productive and which results will come out of it, you need the following kinds of individuals, at a minimum:

1) The people who are involved with creating the actual Web-based app
   This will be primarily the software developers, members of the DevSecOps team, and IT Security, with of course, the Threat Modelers being involved as well.
2) The QA test
   This is an acronym that stands for "Quality Assurance". Toward the end of the development cycle of the Web app project, it will of course have to be tested in order to make sure that it meets the needs of the client. Of course, you will want the Threat Modelers to be involved here as well, to see how the QA testing will stack up to any future Cyber threats.
3) The business goals of the project
   It is important to remember that it will not just be the "geeks" that will be involved in these kinds of meetings. There will also be the business side of the project, and these are the people that will

understand the business perspective of what the client truly wants. This is where the role of the Project Manager will come in, as they will understand the business and requirements of the client the best.

4) Tracking of the project

This is where the project milestones will be captured, and flagged down to make sure that all of them are being met. Rather than having more than manager looking at this (because of the multiple titles of people being involved), it might just be wiser in the end to have the CISO or vCISO oversee this part of the Web application project.

The Decision-Making Process

Although one of the primary goals in any Cybersecurity meeting is to share knowledge and information, one of the other primary objectives as well what the various Calls to Action (CTA) will be. This will of course be reviewed and agreed upon in the meeting. But since Cybersecurity experts and software developers and members of the DevSecOps teams all hold a wealth of knowledge, there will be the risk of course of conflict, and possibly even larger levels of disagreements that could happen. Obviously, this is just human nature, in both our professional and personal lives. And, in both situations, it is important to resolve before they become too hard to handle.

Since Threat Modeling is just one of the components of the overall Project Management efforts, it is very important that the team leader (or even the vCISO or CISO) tries to keep the goals of the Threat Modelers as much aligned as possible with the overall objectives. To help achieve these goals, many IT Security teams use what is called the "RACI" model. It is designed for all of the key stakeholders on meeting, and the following matrix breaks this down further:

TASKS	ARCHITECT	SYSTEMS ADMIN	DEVELOPER	TESTER
Threat Modeling	A		I	I
Security Design Principles	A	I	I	
System Architecture	A	C		
Architecture Design and Review	R			

After this matrix was created, Microsoft launched a version of its own that added two variables to the Threat Modeling role. These Own, Participate, and Validate. It is illustrated in the matrix below.

SESSION	ARCHITECT	PROGRAM MANAGER	SOFTWARE TEST	PENETRATION TEST	DEVELOPER
Requirements	O	O	V	P	V
Software Model	P	P	O	V	O
Threat Enumeration	P	P	V	O	V
Mitigations	P	P	O	V	O
Validate	O	O	P	P	P

Note that in the above two models, the variables are represented as follows:

R = Responsible
A = Approver
C= Consulted
I = Informed
O = Own
P =Participate
V = Validate

The Components of an Effective Threat Modeling Meeting

Apart from the usual obstacles that occur in meetings, one of the other ones that of the meeting objectives. Many times, the dynamics of the meeting can change quite a bit because topics can change quickly. Probably one of the best ways to handle this is simply print out the objectives and make it clear that any deviations from it will not be tolerated by any means whatsoever. Get the meeting done requires a rapid fire succession of items that needs to get done. Also, try to keep it short, about 45 minutes. It would also be quite helpful if the type of meeting is also discussed. For example, is it anyone of the following:

- A decision-making meeting;
- A working meeting;
- Or a review meeting?

A good example of an agenda is as follows:

- The Project Kickoff that succinctly details the objectives to be met from the meeting;
- Any diagramming (or whiteboarding) that is needed;

- Anything new that is happening in the realm the discovery of new Cyber-based variants;
- How these new variants (if any) will be triaged (in this regard, you can come up with a triaging tree).

The ultimate goal of course is collaboration. You want to have everybody more or less on the same page after the meeting so at least you will have some degree of assurance that there will be at team effort, as opposed to the siloed, which was discussed earlier in this book. It is also important to note that overlap in the meeting objectives can also happen. If this is the case, finish each objective of the meeting, then on a whiteboard (or something similar) show the overlap, and why it is important. Also, have a minute taker at these meetings, so that past conversations can be visited again.

Also, make sure that everybody attending this meeting has at least one Call to Action (CTA) that they need to work on and complete before the next meeting. Make sure that the right people have been assigned to what they can logically be accomplished. There is nothing worse than giving something to somebody who has absolutely no idea about doing. Also, it is very important to keep in mind that the words spoken can have profound affects, whether it is for the good or the bad. In other words, don't ever personalize anything, as the intended person can take great offense to it.

Finally, keep these meetings in mind with diversity. For example, rather than bringing in the same people week after week, bring in some outside participants, such as the customers themselves. After all, the project is about them, and the most powerful input you can get will be from this group of people.

At this point, since we have examined conflict at Cyber meetings in some detail now, let us take a step back and examine a real world example of this. This is whether or not to use manual Pen Testing versus automated Pen Testing.

The Penetration Testing Process

Penetration Testing is probably one of the most thorough ways in which to examine where the vulnerabilities and gaps lie in your IT and Network infrastructures. In a way, this can be compared to conducting an angiogram on the human heart. This is the only way to confirm where the blockages are in the coronary arteries. But despite the advantages that Pen Testing can bring to the table, it does suffer from numerous disadvantages as well that may not make the best solution in the end.

For example:

1) They are manually executed:
   Depending on what is required, many Pen Tests require the use of at least two teams, which are known as the Red Team and the

Blue Team. The former takes the role and mindset of an actual Cyberattacker, in which the lines of defenses at your business are broken down. But this of course is done in an ethical and legal manner, with contracts being signed ahead of time before the actual engagement. It is important to note here that while a small portion of a Pen Test is automated, a bulk of it done on a manual basis, especially if you are using these teams to do it. Because of this, conflicts could arise among the group members, and because of this, the ultimate goal of meeting the needs of the client may not be best achieved.

2) Scheduling conflicts:
Apart from the team issues, there could also be conflicts when it comes to scheduling. For example, if the Pen Testing organization has a strong brand reputation, it is quite likely that could overbook client engagements. As a result, scheduled time could be bumped down to a later time, or worst yet, it is quite possible that you could be waiting months'on end in order to firm up a date for a Pen Test to be conducted at your business. And in the world of the Cyber Threat Landscape, there is not one minute to be lost so that you do not become a victim of a malicious payload.

3) It can be expensive:
Despite the old saying of "You get what you pay for", it is well known that a complete Pen Test (that is conducted manually) can be quite expensive, thus causing many businesses to think twice if this something that is of high priority. The average cost of a Pen Test can range anywhere from $4000.00 to over $100,000.00. Keep in mind that there are certain variables which determine the ultimate cost, and these are as follows:

- The size of your company:
  Obviously, the smaller is the size of your organization in terms of employees, the lower the cost will be.
- The complexity of the test:
  Let's face it, protecting the digital assets of your organization can take a lot of risk controls. This is what makes deciding what should be tested even more difficult. The bottom line is that the more you want examined from a Pen Test, the cost will drive up even further immediately.
- The methodology that is being used:
  Pen Testing is not a one size fits all approach. There are different kinds of testing procedures and tools that can be used. Of course, if you are going to be using multiple testing models with the most sophisticated tools, the overall cost of the Pen Test will go up with just a bat of your eye.

- The experience:
  Just like in a law firm, the most experienced attorneys are going to cost a lot, lot more than the associate ones. So, if you are using Pen Testers with a substantial amount of experience and training, this will cost much more than say, a junior Pen Tester.
- The kind of testing that will be done:
  Typically, most manual Pen Testing is done from the threats are coming from the external environment. But it can also be done for the environment that exists within your business, and this is known as Internal Testing. While doing just one of them can be expensive, attempting to do both will be at least 2x as much, if not more.
- After the Pen Test:
  After testing is done, the Pen Testing team will deliver to you a report of what it has discovered in terms of the weaknesses, gaps, and vulnerabilities that it has found. After that, technically their job is done. But how do remediate all of these? Well guess what… if you want further advice on the corrective actions that need to be taken, that will also drive up the total cost of the Pen Test.
- It is a time-consuming process:
  A thorough Pen Test that is manually conducted can take quite a bit of time to accomplish. Typically, they can last for up to a few weeks, or even longer. Keep in mind that while you are spending time doing this, new threat variants will emerge very quickly, and can impact your business as the Pen Test exercise is being conducted. For this reason alone, many organizations that choose this type of Pen Testing route only do it once a year. But, this is simply not enough in order to keep up with the dynamics of the Cyber Threat Landscape.

AUTOMATED PENETRATION TESTING AND ITS BENEFITS

Is there a solution to the weaknesses that are presented by manual Pen Testing? Yes, there is, and it is actually automated Pen Testing. Using this kind of approach, the need to have the human element involved in the actual process is often eradicated, of course with the exception of presenting the findings and coming up with the corrective actions to the client.

Here are some of the key advantages of automated Pen Testing:

1) It saves time:

   Just imagine all the time it takes to get a Pen Testing team put together to conduct the analyses that are needed at your business. Not only that, but it also takes time to fully assess the environment of the client, and deciding what really needs to get tested. Then, more time is needed in determining the specific tools that will be needed to conduct the required test. But with an automated Pen Test, no time is wasted. You basically plug in the permutations of what needs to be tested, and off the system goes to find those gaps and vulnerabilities. Best of all, the final report is also automatically compiled, so there is no time wasted with that either.

2) It is far less expensive:

   Since the human element is almost taken out, the costs of actually launching and executing an automated Pen Test exercise is far cheaper than the other alternative. In fact, the pricing points that are associated with this are within the budgetary grasps of the Small- to Medium-Sized (SMB) market, which is often an overlooked market segment by the Cybersecurity Industry. For point of comparison, it costs only a few hundred dollars to do an automated Pen Testing exercise, versus the thousands of dollars with the manual process, which is illustrated earlier in this chapter. The costs in this instance are driven primarily by the total number of IP Addresses and/or website domains that need to be scanned and assessed.

3) Scheduling is a lot easier:

   As it was reviewed earlier, one of the main issues of the manual Pen Test are the scheduling conflicts that can arise due to heavy demand for the service, or even trying to get the right Pen Testers in place to do the job. With the automated approach, there is nothing to worry about this. You simply let your Managed Service Provider (MSP) know when you want your Pen Testing to be done, and it will happen, no questions asked.

4) There is no biasness involved:

   One of the key tenets when conducting a Pen Testing drill is for the testers to remain as neutral as possible, so that they can deliver an objective report to the client. But once again, conflicts can arise with the team members, thus causing this biasness to actually happen, which can impact the outcome that is presented. With using the automated Pen Testing processes, this problem is 100% eradicated, as many of the tools that are used are based upon the open source concept, which allows the analyses to be vendor neutral. As a benefit of this, the reports that are compiled for the client are also unbiased, and even more importantly, are consistent. This allows for the client to take the path that they need to in terms of utilizing the best remediative actions possible.

5) Tests can be run at any time:

Probably one of the best advantages of automated Pen Testing is that it can be run at any time you want them to, unlike the manual way, where it is only done 1x a year because of the prohibitive costs. In fact, with the automated approach, you can run tests on a 24 X 7 X 365 basis, and even run different kinds of Pen Tests simultaneously. This is truly one of the best approaches that you can when trying to keep one step (preferably even more) of the Cyberattacker. Also remember that humans are prone to fatigue over a long period of time, which can increase the error rate of the tests that are being conducted. Automated software tools do not suffer from this setback.

6) It can be updated quickly:

The tools that are used in automated Pen Testing can be quickly updated to reflect the latest advancements that are occurring. This stands in total opposition to the time and expense it would take to educate your Pen Testers and bring them up to speed with the latest trends that are occurring.

The Cybersecurity Threat Landscape is constantly changing on a minute-by-minute basis, and because of that, companies simply cannot keep up with fighting off the threat variants. Even if a manual Pen Test was to be done, as also mentioned, there will be newer attack vectors that come out, even when the Pen Testing exercise is being conducted. Thus, this defeats the purpose of doing it all together.

But with making use of automated Pen Testing, you will know where your gaps, vulnerabilities, and weaknesses lie on a real-time basis. Thus, you can take steps to mitigate risks on the spot, on a real-time basis, and not after the fact.

Finally, one other trend to be on the lookout for is that of Artificial Intelligence (AI) and Machine Learning (ML). These technologies will allow the software tools to even learn and make human-like judgments as to what needs to be examined next as the automated Pen Testing is being carried out.

HOW TO CARRY OUT THREAT MODELING IN THE SOFTWARE DEVELOPMENT LIFECYCLE

In the world of software development, there are many kinds and types of methodologies that can be used to meet the development needs of the client, as well as to ensure that the project is done on time and most important, under budget. But once again, although the predominant crew here will be the software developers, you cannot count out the DevSecOps and even the IT Security teams, which will include even the Threat Modelers. One of their roles could even be possibly playing what if scenarios in order to make sure that the source code, which is developed, is as strong as possible, and can even possibly withstand a security if it was ever faced with one. In this subsection of this chapter, we look at various methodologies, and how Threat Modeling can play a role in them.

It is important to note that all of these methodologies fall under the main branch of what is known as the "Software Development Lifecycle" or "SDLC" for short.

The Waterfall Methodology

This is a software methodology that emulates the flow of a waterfall. It can be technically defined as follows:

> The waterfall methodology is a linear project management approach, where stakeholder and customer requirements are gathered at the beginning of the project, and then a sequential project plan is created to accommodate those requirements. The waterfall model is so named because each phase of the project cascades into the next, following steadily down like a waterfall.
>
> *(SOURCE: https://www.projectmanager.com/guides/*
> *waterfall-methodology)*

With this kind of methodology, Threat Modeling can be used in the following stages:

1) The requirements stage;
2) The design stage;
3) The testing phase (this is also where the QA process also starts as well).

In the first two stages, you are actually developing and creating the source code, and hopefully, your software development team is also checking for bugs. If there is a bug, then that is also a direct threat to the application especially, if it goes unresolved. In the last part, which is testing, you are affirming that all of the bugs are ironed out, and there are no obvious threats to the system. But this is no guarantee obviously, as threats can still linger around, and even go unnoticed. It is here, at this stage, that you may way to do both a Pen Test and a Threat Hunting exercise to absolutely make sure there still in existence. In this regard, you are checking for any covert backdoors that are well hidden intentional or not.

So, how can Threat Modeling work here? Well, if you are making use of project-based milestones, which are also "gates", you insert a permutation into the Waterfall Methodology by stating that you cannot move further ahead until the bugs are totally eradicated, with the help of Pen Testing and Threat Hunting/Modeling. Just imagine at each module if there were hundreds of bugs (which if theoretically possible), in each module. You would not be able to move ahead onwards with the milestones until the preceding has been totally 100% taken care of.

Just think of it this way: If you are totally free of bugs at each step of the development process, then that means once again on a theoretical basis) you are free from all sorts of threats.

The Agile Methodology

In actuality, this is the methodology that is the probably used most by software development teams. It can be technically defined as follows:

> Agile software development refers to software development methodologies centered around the idea of iterative development, where requirements and

solutions evolve through collaboration between self-organizing cross-functional teams. The ultimate value in Agile development is that it enables teams to deliver value faster, with greater quality and predictability and greater aptitude to respond to change. Scrum and Kanban are two of the most widely used Agile methodologies.

(SOURCE: https://www.cprime.com/resources/
what-is-agile-what-is-scrum/)

So as you can see from the above definition, the idea of the Agile Methodology is that you keep repeating each step until it is perfect to move onto the next one. The idea here is to deliver the project deliverables in much smaller chunks to the client, rather than have them to wait for the deliverable final to be produced. Even if you use this kind of approach, the Threat Modeler has to be literally on standby to help around for threats that could very well emerge from here. This allows the Threat Modeler to jump from one kind of milestone to another in this specific regard.

One area in Threat Modeling that is particularly useful is in a test-driven, design environment. Here, along with the software development team, you develop a series of tests and preconditions that are very carefully evaluated at first. Then, you have serious discussions as to which each source code model will do. By following these traditional rules, this will allow for both the Threat Modeler and your software development team to critically think about the potential security threats are, and how to even make best use cases out of them. But it is important to keep in mind that if you are using this kind of software methodology to build out your Web application project and from there find the potential threat variants, you will actually need to have two kinds of models, which are as follows:

• The model of the software itself;
• A model of the threats themselves.

To accomplish the above task, you can use a technique that is known as "Whiteboarding". This is literally what it sounds like, in that you take a whiteboard, and draw out both models. Of course, it will be important to save both, and you can do this quite easily with the camera of your wireless device. You can also make use of other more well-established techniques such as that of "YAGNI" (which was discussed at the beginning of this chapter) or even what is known as the "Elevation of Privilege".

VALUING YOUR THREAT MODELERS

When you undertake a huge Project Management task, it is by no doubt a complex process, with many moving parts to it. And of course, there is a direct correlation here: The more complex it becomes, the more people can get involved, and there is the effect of overcrowding. Then, the realization becomes whose word is more important, and which one carries more weight? This is of course a very difficult question to answer, as there are many factors here at play. But the worst part of this is that these are all qualitative components that are even harder to understand, because so much of this based upon psychology.

Very often, this will leave a feeling of being undervalued, and thus not want to contribute to the team anymore. But the one thing to keep them motivated is to tell this: "For every bug that is found, that is a new threat discovered. And of course you and I know that there is no such thing as a 100% bug free environment". All of this should lead up to a feeling of importance to the Threat Modeler, thus fueling their motivation even more so to do the best job that I can.

MEASURING THE OVERALL VALUE OF THREAT HUNTING

In our world today, success or failure is dependent primarily upon meeting or exceeding Key Performance Indicators (also known as "KPIs"), and other such types of metrics, whether we like it or not. As humans, we hate it when we know that we have done the best that we can, but we still fail because we did not meet some sort of metric. This is probably exemplified by the "road warrior", who is the sales rep. If they don't meet their sales quota for a certain quarter, the chances are fairly high that their job could be in jeopardy. But to some degree or another, in the world of Cyber, most professionals here in this arena don't have to deal with metrics, because it so difficult to put a metric or even a KPI on a threat variant. Probably the only ones that are used so far are those that relate to how long it takes to detect a threat to actually responding to it.

And it is in this same fashion that it is hard to evaluate your Threat Modeler just based upon some KPIs or metrics, which really are pretty useless in the end. But unfortunately in the end, you being the vCISO or the CISO, you have to somehow or another explain to the other members of the C-Suite and/or even the Board of Directors just what kind of value that your Threat Modeling team is bringing to the business. One obvious answer is that what the future Threat Landscape looks like, and that is needed to keep tweaking your lines of defenses.

To help you out in this goal, some time ago, Microsoft came up with a model with what is known technically as the "Microsoft SDL Threat Modeling Tool". This is demonstrated in the matrix below:

RATING	COMMENTS
0 – No Threat Model Present	Unacceptable
1 – Not Acceptable	Out of date by design or document age
2 – OK	*DFD with tangible assets such as data stores, data flows, and trust boundaries *At least one threat per asset *Mitigations for threats above a certain risk level
3 – Good	Meets the OK and most threats have been and/or are being mitigated
4 – Excellent	Meets the good bar, and also: *All STRIDE threats have been identified mitigated, and other external threats have been identified *Customer facing Cyber documents are available for quick usage

WHEN DOES THREAT MODELING END IN THE PROJECT MANAGEMENT OR SDLC?

Just like all things in life, the Software Development Lifecycle (SDLC) does eventually come to an end. It may be just a few months, or it could even go on for a year so, it all depends upon the magnitude and scope of the work that needs to get done. Of course you know the project will be officially done once it has handed off to the customer. But the next question that will come into mind is when the does the work of the Threat Modeler actually end? In the world of Cybersecurity, we know the work never ends, and it will never end. That is just the nature of the work of the work that is involved.

But when it comes to the Project Management team and efforts, when does the Threat Modeler actually call it quits? Well, this is primarily based upon two key factors, which are as follows:

- Can the Threat Modeling activity involved be viewed as a separate activity?
- How deep was the Threat Modeler involved in the project?

Obviously, these two questions are literally intertwined with each other. For example, if the Threat Modeler was deep into the project at hand, then it cannot be viewed as a separate activity. But if he or she (or even the entire Threat Modeling team) was involved for just a short duration, then it can be viewed as a separate activity. But in the end, it all comes down to the client. If the Project Manager goes into detail to some degree about the kind of Cyber testing that was done, they may want to retain that Threat Modeler on a contract basis – after all finding a good Threat Modeler these days is still no easy task, as there are not too many of them out there, at least not yet.

But back to the old mantra: Bugs will always be found, even in the software upgrades and patches that are found. These also will need to be investigated, because from here, even newer threat variants can be formulated. These are technically known as "Zero Day Attacks", because nobody else even knows about them yet. But to discover them, you need to a good Threat Hunter on hand to look at these variants, to predict what variants that emerge from these Zero Day attacks will look like.

ANOTHER WAY TO MEASURE THREAT MODELING SUCCESS

Earlier in this chapter, it was discussed how Key Performance Indicators (KPIs) and other metrics are used to gauge an employee's overall success in their job. While it is useful in some industries more than others, it is hard to put a quantitative number for Cybersecurity. As it was also mentioned, the Cyber Threat Landscape is always changing, so even if you could put numbers to employees, it won't be effective for very long. Probably the best way is the qualitative way. Simply put, you ask for feedback from the Project Manager, the IT Security Manager, or even the vCISO and/or CISO themselves as to how they think that the Threat Modelers have done in their last assignment. But in the end, it is the first two titles that will give you the most valuable input

- After each milestone in the project management, a plan has been completed;
- Immediately after finding a big in the source code during the development of the Web application project.

The most effective type of feedback will be with the second one. That is because software bugs are not a planned activity, and you can get a true gauge as to how your Threat Modeler did. For example, some of the questions that you can ask include the following:

- How proactive was he or she when the software bug was first discovered?
- How was the advice when it came time to remediate that specific software bug?
- Were they quick enough to collect intel about the software bug and trying to predict what future ones could look like throughout the course of the SDLC?

Some of the more general types of questions that you can also ask include the following about your Threat Modeler, or the team that they belonged in:

- What was truly effective that he or she really did?
- What could they have done better in the software bug detection and variant modeling processes?
- What other types of additional tasks can the Threat Modeler take on to improve upon and hone in their respective skills?

WHO LEADS THE THREAT MODELING TEAM?

Whenever anybody imagines the IT Security team, one often thinks of people working together, in order beef up the lines of defenses for the company they work at. But as it has been mentioned throughout this book, this is far from the reality. Many of the IT Security teams still remain disjointed as ever before, and in fact, many of them still in work in siloes in this regard. This simply means that people on the IT Security team often just work in their own groups of a few people, or just a few people. This can also be said of the Threat Modeler. They don't even work with others; they sit at their desk all day, pouring over information and data, to try to predict the future.

So you may be asking at this point, being the vCISO or the CISO, just how can you break down these silos so that the IT Security team can work as one cohesive unit, and most importantly, get the Threat Modelers involved also? After all, your team needs their valuable insight to predict what the future of the Cyber Threat Landscape could look like:

1. Give everyone a seat at the Cyber table:
   This means the entire team and everybody, not just a select few.
2. Integrate risk into processes:
   Risk is at the crux of anything and everything related to Cybersecurity. If relevant to the situation at hand, this topic must be discussed with everybody.
3. Introduce a risk management survey:
   As the CISO or vCISO, take the bold move and give employee of your IT Security team a survey to fill out, asking them what steps are needed from you to break down the walls of siloes. For the best feedback, don't give out multiple choice questions. Make them all essay, so you get the most honest feedback possible.
4. Build trust and relationships with respect:
   This is probably the hardest, but yet most important thing that can be done. Always treat members, especially your Threat Modelers, the way you want to be treated. Sounds antiquated, but it does really work in the end.
5. Communicate:
   This is also hard to accomplish, along with respect. But this has to be accomplished. Hold team meetings at least once a week, and if possible have quarterly outdoor meetings in a very casual, and fun like environment.

WIDELY USED THREAT MODELING TECHNIQUES

So far in this chapter, we have introduced various techniques that the CISO or the vCISO can use in order to introduce the concept of Threat Modeling as well as that team in a positive way. After all of this is said and done, more than likely you will be asked as to what kind of Threat Models you use. Well, we address some of this in this subsection of this chapter.

1) The Stride Model:
   This was created in 1999 and utilized by Microsoft in 2002, STRIDE is the most, widely regarded threat-modeling method of today. An example of this is seen below:

THREAT	PROPERTY VIOLATED	THREAT DEFINITION
Spoofing Identity	Authentication	Mimicking another identity
Data Tampering	Integrity	Modifying data on the disk, or memory, or anywhere else it may reside at
Repudiation	Non-Repudiation	Claiming that you did not do a certain event
Information Disclosure	Confidentiality	Giving access to data to someone when they are not allowed to have it
Denial of Service	Availability	Running out of resources to do a job task
Privilege Escalation	Authorization	Allowing somebody to do a certain task that they are not allowed to do

It is important to note that the STRIDE model has been successfully applied to many types and kinds of real-world Cyberattacks and events.

2) The LINDDUN Model:
   This is an acronym that stands for Linkability, Identifiability, Nonrepudiation, Detectability, Disclosure of Information, Unaware-ness, and Noncompliance. This is more designed for data privacy, and is especially useful for coming into compliance with the data privacy laws of the GDPR, CCPA, HIPAA, etc. It is illustrated below:

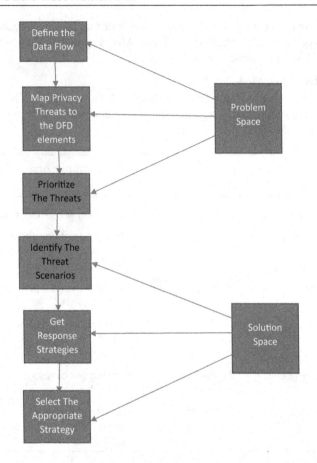

LINDDUN first starts with a Data Flow Diagram of the system, which defines the data flows, data stores, and external processes. By analyzing them from the point of view of threat categories, this model can identify a threat's applicability to the system and build threat trees.

3) The CVSS:

This is an acronym that stands for The Common Vulnerability Scoring System (CVSS). It captures the major functions of vulnerability and yields a numerical severity score. CVSS was developed by the NIST and is now kept up to date by the Forum of Incident Response and Security Teams (FIRST) with support and contributions from the CVSS Special Interest Group. This framework provides users a common and standardized scoring system for different types and kinds of Cyber-based threats.

4) The Attack Trees:

Attack trees are diagrams that emulate threat variants in a tree form. The tree root is the starting point for the attack, and the leaves are ways to achieve that goal. Each goal is represented as a separate tree. The end result is a set of attack trees.

For example, attack trees can be built for each threat variant. Administrators can build attack trees and use them to make security decisions; determine whether the systems are vulnerable to a Cyberattack; and review and give feedback on a specific type of attack.

5) The Quantitative Threat Modeling Method:

This hybrid method consists of attack trees, STRIDE, and CVSS methods applied in synergy. The first step in this process is build attack trees for the five threat categories of STRIDE. This activity shows the dependencies among attack the various attack. After that, the CVSS method is applied and scores are calculated for the threats in the tree.

SOURCES FOR CHAPTER 5

1) Adam Shostack, "Threat Modeling: Designing For Security", Wiley, 2015.

Conclusions

6

Overall, this book has covered the theme of what the Zero Trust Framework is all about, as well as its limitations and advantages. The Cyber Threat Landscape is changing at a very fast pace, and thus, it is very important to try to keep up as much as possible. Other security solutions have been tried and for the most part have failed, especially that of the Perimeter Defense Model, which was also reviewed in detail in this book.

We need a newer solution that is unique, cutting edge, as well as scalable for the long term. This is where the Zero Trust Framework comes into play. This has been viewed as an extreme sort of methodology by both society and business, because in it, nobody can be trusted whatsoever, from either the internal or the external environments. But wherever it has been deployed, there has been some proven success with it, as it has helped to greatly reduce the statistical probability of being impacted by a Cyberattack.

But even here, the Zero Trust Framework is not without its own set of flaws, especially in the following areas:

- Still using hackable forms of Multifactor Authentication (MFA);
- The repeated need to be authenticated over and over again;
- The possibilities of having the information and data transmitted from the Authentication Server to the Shared Resources Server being tampered with, and the integrity compromised.

We offered three distinct solutions for these flaws, which are as follows:

- Making use of Biometrics as the only form of MFA tools. In this regard, the use of Fingerprint Recognition, Iris Recognition, and Facial Recognition were introduced.
- The use of Privileged Access Management (PAM) as an alternative to avoid having to be authenticated and authorized over and over again.

DOI: 10.1201/9781003392965-6

- Making use of the concepts of Quantum Mechanics and Quantum Cryptography as a means to protect the integrity of the transmissions from the Authentication Server to the Shared Resources Server.

At this point, it is important to review the highlights of what was covered in each chapter of this book:

Chapter 1: Introduction

Chapter 2:

- The Password
- The Rise of Two-Factor Authentication
- Multifactor Authentication
- An Introduction to Biometrics
- Definition and Unique Features
- The Process of Identification
- Other Important Concepts
- The Biometric Sensor
- A Review of Fingerprint Recognition
- A Review of Facial Recognition
- Iris Recognition

Chapter 3:

- An Overview of the Public Key Infrastructure (PKI)
- What It Is All About
- A Review into Biocryptography
- Biocryptography and Virtual Private Networks
- The Hashing Mechanism

Chapter 4:

- The Origins of the Zero Trust Framework
- Zero Trust Framework & Quantum Mechanics
- The Demise of Perimeter Security
- The Emergence of the Zero Trust Framework
- The Basic Zero Trust Framework Model
- The Advantages of the Zero Trust Framework
- The Disadvantages of the Zero Trust Framework
- Some of the Best Practices
- The Flaws with the Traditional Zero Trust Framework Model
- The Use of Biometrics

- The Weakness of Repeated Authorization and Authentication
- The Strains of on Prem PAM
- Why PAM Is Better Suited for the Cloud
- The Advantages of Using PAM In The Cloud
- A Best Practices Guide for Deploying a PAM-Based Solution
- The Mistakes That Are Made When Deploying PAM Solutions and How to Fix Them
- The Importance of Just in Time (JIT) Access
- The Four Pillars to PAM Success
- The Finer Points of Privileged Access Management
- The Use of Quantum Mechanics In Our Proposed Model of the Zero Trust Framework
- Quantum Cryptography
- The Literature Review
- The Quantum Key Distribution Center (QKDC)
- The Photon Particle Array Structures
- Our Proposed Zero Trust Framework Model

Chapter 5:

- What Exactly Is Threat Modeling?
- The Process Involved in Threat Modeling
- Making the Case for Threat Modeling
- How to Have Quality-Based Threat Modeling Meetings
- How to Carry Out Threat Modeling in the Software Development Lifecycle
- Valuing Your Threat Modelers
- Measuring the Overall Value of Threat Hunting
- When Does Threat Modeling End in the Project Management or SDLC?
- Another Way to Measure Threat Modeling Success
- Who Leads the Threat Modeling Team?
- Widely Used Threat Modeling Techniques

Remember, the Zero Trust Framework is a methodology that is meant to provide the highest levels of security of the internal environment of your business. Therefore, you and your IT Security team need to conduct regular Threat Hunting and Threat Modeling exercises in order to make sure that there no malicious threat actors in this environment.

It is important to keep in mind as well is that the Zero Trust Framework is not a "one size fits all" solution. Instead, as its name points, it is merely a framework from which a business has to fit, mold, and adopt to its own security requirements and environment. In other words, what works for one organization will not necessarily work for the other. Therefore, a lot of time and planning has to take place on the Zero Trust Framework that is most appropriate for you and your employees.

Speaking of which, apart from deploying the Zero Trust Framework in preplanned stages, it is also very important that you get the buy in from your employees. After all in the end, change is something that most humans don't like to endure, and because of that, you need to have open lines of communications with them as each step of your Zero Trust Framework is being deployed. If you do not get their buy in, they will be very hesitant to use it (or not even use at all), thus defeating its purpose entirely. Not just your employees, but every key stakeholder involved in your company must be informed as well.

Always be patient with the deployment of your Zero Trust Framework Model. It won't happen overnight, and in fact, if it is planned properly, it can take as long as a year until (or even more) it is fully deployed.

Finally, the question gets asked is if one day the Zero Trust Framework will make the password obsolete. The password has been around for quite a long time, and it never seems like that it will go away in the long term. But the potential for this to happen does exist, and the technology even is available today to make this a reality, as it was discussed throughout this book with the use of Biometric Technology. In the end, it all comes down to how much society really wants to change and improve their current levels of security.

As just stated, humans are by nature, very resistant to change, and are happy staying with the status quo, even if that change is for something better. This is the main hurdle that will need to be overcome if we are truly destined to become a password less society. The tools are in place – we just have to see the benefits of it and accept it in the end.

Index

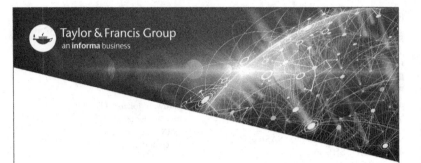